D.F.L.
LIT

Cover photo: Jerry Pena

Cover design: Mike Corrao

The five images: Celestial Subliminals

Book design by D.F.L.

www.dfllit.com

contact@dfllit.com

THE WORLD DREAMER

Michael Borth

To be read in the order of your choosing.

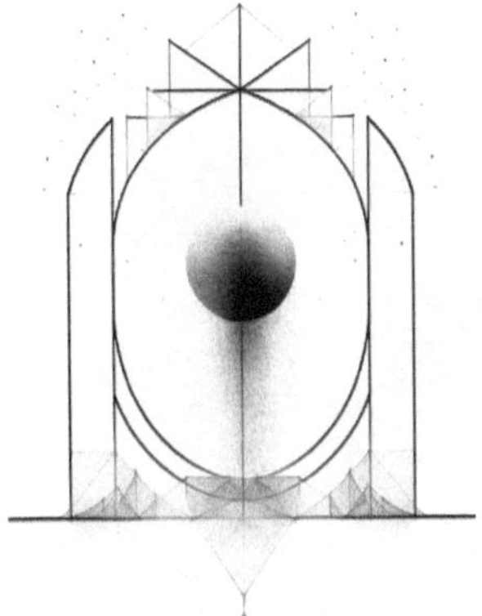

Book 0
Turn the page.

Book 1
Page 109

Book 2
Page 249

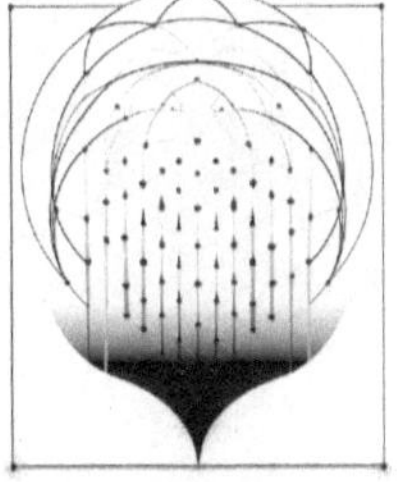

Book 3
Page 333

The Ruins

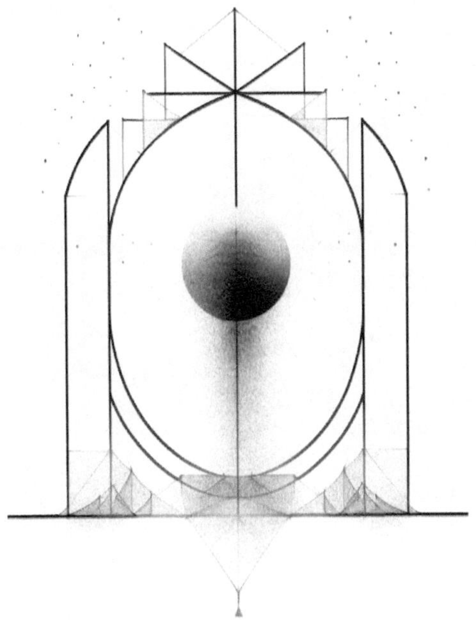

Book 0
The Past, Water
Initiates: The Path of Openings
Centers: Crete, São Paulo
Threshold: The Illuminated Stranger

THE MAN WHO WILL WATCH MY CAR

I am going to pay a man
to stand by my car
and protect it
from the nomadic thieves
of the grid deserts,
the car I dreamed about
when I was a child
when I was unemployed
when I was weeping
in small painted rooms
with my hands in a ring.

But the man will be handsome
and my wife will begin to notice
his mountainous hands
his stoic postures
his black coffee
the outline of the gun
he bought with mercenary earnings
in a lush hotel room
in Athens or Istanbul.

In our narrow austere building
she will seek in the day
views and glances
that warm her tree of centers
as he stands not sweating
in the heat
we still bargain with.

And one day
when I have just stopped crushing an orange
I will hear her whimper
and the whimper
I will hear
all over my life,
a sonic marking
a final admission
and we both will know
but diagram our routines

and watch our glacial dances
turn the very life
we now detest.

And the whimper
will find a lost brother
in the persistent click
coming from the undercarriage
of my wheeled treasure
and my mechanic
will want me to help his son
in a business matter
seemingly drawn
by foaming mental defectives
in a room of one light
and falling snow.

And my boss,
a pale man who gnaws his upper lip,
will ask me obscene questions
about my car
and we will go on night rides
where he talks of his mistress,
the one who cannot
bear condoms,
and he will view his life
as a series of growing prisons
where every escape
is an entrance
and the pulse
from the birth of each streetlight
will make us slow
and melancholic
will make us remember
microwaved pizza
and adolescent loves
as bleedingmen
organize their trash.

THE ROOMS TO COME

Whistling that comes down
the vertical corridor
along with a green olive
and a pink ball.

There is a perfect place
out by the archetype gas station
where an old man stands
in a puddle of flowers,
crying pink,
not far from the abandoned
drive-in movie screen
in invisible flames
in some perpetual dusk.

I find it
and stare at it
past what can be seen
and make myself
unable to be found,
shedding voices
and wandering
through some other city
vanished and serene,
touching the coins
on the table, on the wall unit,
becoming beyond real
and beyond imaginary.

Coughing and the infinite sneeze
and a troubled dog,
the incomprehensible tiendas
like the one with golden shoes.
The punks that lived
in the house they haunted
by the fruit stand
where my mother treated me
to Slim Jims.
And we all wondered
why I was so fat.

The drawer of expired condoms
on election day in Brazil,
the tissue box that says Elite,
the careful drawings
of nonexistent cities
I kept in a desk.
We live in the dreams
that we received
and changed
and dreamed again.

A rabid childhood collage
fed to a river
and collected
in a distant sea
and eaten, now a psychotic,
and vomited
on the shore
where it is eaten
by a fawn
that we kill and devour
ten years later,
and in the feast
we are visited
by an exact copy
of the room we are now in
and a vision taste
of all rooms to come.

THE WOODEN BOX

When I touch her in the AC I remember the body I made
long ago, maybe after school, when I was free with records
and bad weed. She says I like. We never got açaí
below the carnaval banners, with the drumming kids.

The cat came into the apartment and trashed my clothes.
Afraid of the sound of motorcycles, because here come the thieves.
I want to stop dreaming about big complicated cities at night.
My friend is waiting for a new lover, but she only wants a foot rub.

Three statues of monks and the bodies writhe about the
abandoned church, the breeze like fallen hair. Several people
saw the same deer, together in the dark
of the meditation, gathered about the monitor
for the results of my latest STD test, we use Google Translate
to speak gonorrhea, and chicken pox. One dispenser
com açúcar, one without, tall tubes for the empties.

I love my grandparents more each day, I miss the blintzes
and the six o'clock special, and I miss *The Price Is Right*
in the Ragú afternoons—you know I never wanted
to be like this, and I was called a whore in my own dream.
Old World Style, man on gondola.

Using your hands to open a wooden box containing your hand,
and using your hands to discover if it is the left or the right,
and when you realize which one the real hand disappears,
you drop the box, and you keep playing... and playing...
humming old songs.

A LITTLE TASTE OF PRISON

The trees extend in the echo fountain
it will get better and better and better...
Reaching through the blonde dirt and through the seeds
like purple coalshells like armored worms.
Power surges of ecstasy but I will run and collapse
in the dark house-memories and the long doubt
as you will run from what you fear you can do.

Light pouring from your eyes to make the world
that made the light and the eyes.
The song and smoke from everywhere
matching your peaks and promising the great range
of everhigher peaks, the realization is a body
growing inside you, larger than your body,
god needs your body (to get a little taste of prison),
and the winds will guide you to withstand the winds
as you follow an evolution and are made to stand,
shaking in the only time to birth and receive
the current of corridors
of hanging moss and rockpattern
through your navel.

It is desperate and wry, magical and shimmering and bored,
making your skin clear, asking itself through you
to increase audacity and brilliance in the best and only game that ever was,
down the repeating spherical hall of every direction,
because there is nowhere else to go.

VAPORLANDS

Big sad South American cities
where there are sudden cuts of jungle
and the walls weep
and everything has been blasted
by the moisture
so there is tired moss and shadow
and the newer apartment buildings
look older and wiser
than any stone ruin.

São Paulo is the city
where people peer into blackened windows
and in Da Nang
a child would always appear
to smile
and in Lisbon
it was the city of secret construction
or abandoned projects,
and through the empty windowframes
slanted wooden beams
were saved and exalted
by channels of sunlight.

We are given clues
to our own childhood—
a zen sandbox,
a recurring staircase—
working backward
to be born head out
in a white-tiled café
where the coffee is poured
from a strong kettle
whose scrollwork
has been partially erased
and the opera singer's father
kept finding new women
even though the church
finally let him become
a Roman Catholic preacher.

The segments of digital numbers
float above your palm
free from their plastic houses,
the man will not be let back into the bar
and the shutter is already halfclosed,
the astrologer in Medellín
keeps posting videos
and the more beautiful she becomes
the more she is talking
only to you.

THE ORGAN GRINDER

It's sad that we live in the grass
of the earth of the unsaid. Isn't every reason
a manicured lie? On Saturdays
they have tripe.

Bury me in the beige
uniform of the organ grinder.
Does there always have to be one
beautiful woman working
at every single eatery? You'll find,
drunk at a bar (near your friend's farm),
that an excess of love
was always your problem.
All you have to do
is find someone who agrees.
All you have to do
is stop screaming
at the breeding consultant.

THE CITY OF YOUR BIRTH

A man will come to you
perhaps
during the siesta of the modem.
The city of your birth
will bear the name of his ancestors
and he will take you to a buffet
where the great pianist sits
with food in his teeth.

In the room where you stay
the paintings that surround you
will become more familiar
will fit some personal museum
will hold clues
in the charged district
where the buses shake the loft
where the Hotel Palace Mienda
stands like a rust answer
to the question asked
by the remembered child
who makes lines of soldiers
on the roots of a tree
on the shore of the lake.

The sky is destined
to fill with falcons
and the rodents will be pierced,
twisted in scarlet,
and sold in an underground flea
where the blind live
in a constellation of braille.

There comes a time
when you can no longer count
all the madmen,
and the night the new criminal
is cloaked in peacock feathers
a lone man howls
from the navel of the apartment buildings.
Then, a blast of tubas.

BETA BURNS

The age of beta burns
and drunk girlfriends'
drunk boyfriends,

Dad going to the store for strawberries.
200 acres for sale
and dead kids outside Denver.

The welcome mat
has become part of the brick
and the horses are wearing great
bandage-colored masks,
blind, eating grass.

Saint Augustine
and the blue breastmilk
of not the women but of God.
I wondered, hungover at the Kingston bar,
how many parts of life
find us unconscious and at the breast,
receiving gifts we do not yet understand,
that are not even memory.
So we are left to always look back
to find each mother
and to find each milk.

THE DAY OF TWINS

There were so many twins yesterday
I had to laugh,
and who woke me up this morning
with their operatic practice?

When we meet at the cinema
we both begin to cough.

Isn't it amazing the golden nightstreets
in my memory, each tree a heavy
layer of
[Latin for "pads

and membranes"],

the alopecia of the ironbar of the window,
painted over, proof in the halted drops,
the yellow can of tonic, the fact of Belorussia,

and in the back of her car
we stop at the whitening
from every headlight.

The Ruins

EASTER

The shopping cart asks me
if I will help stop coupon fraud
and the Mobil station clerk
tells me his family is missing
after the bombings in Sri Lanka.
On the screen:
white text and wreckage.

In the corner of the parking lot
I smoke cigarettes from Peru,
home again
in the falling pink petals
of a cherry blossom tree.

DUMB AND DUMBER

Her throat had been cut
and I turned her in the scarce light
to examine the scar
as she told me of the two men
that attacked her
on a street in Saigon.
We had met in a bar
where I vowed not to move
and there was some Mountain
Dew promotion—
cups of green and vodka.
When we scoffed
at some loud Australian,
she said, He looks like
Dumb and Dumber.

The woman who said
my head was Brahminshaped
had been impregnated
after her first blood
but she fell in love
with a sick man in a European capital
but was here now again
in the Himalayan foothills
with her drunk husband—
wet and red eyes.

I love a woman
when her laughter
cannot be forgotten,
real laughter,
that holy capacity
that is so rare
and comes bigger
than a roving storm
over the western coast of Italy
where we all stopped our eating
to marvel
at the long grey channel
and its falling glitter.

The Ruins

A profile of lips
and the automated voices
of the fruit vendors.

WHAT THEY FAIL TO KEEP

Hands in the waterfire
that is also a burning bush
a tumbleweed aflame
a nervous system ignited.

Rummaging and culling
and collecting and washing
save keep discard and leave—
the hands going.
Simple divisions. Like with Like.
Opposites and antonyms
and what the eye makes a border of.
Collisions and waves of order
though the categories will not stop,
quick ambitions in the melt and shift

though now the skin is a doorway to bone
and the hands begin to merge
with what they fail to keep.

HONG KONG NIGHTCLUB

It is always a Hong Kong nightclub
and there is always the scarred one
who could only be a henchman
pushing on her arm and nodding.
I know she was turned on.
In the rain we look for dim sum.

It is rumored my dad almost had his own show.
And my stepcousin was on a show
and Solange almost had her own show
after the other show.
I pull on my new beerbelly and I wonder:
when will I have my own show?

Diogenes in Alexander's shadow.
In dark Vietnamese coffeehouses
we arrange letters using our thumbs.
We have finally become cheap with our hearts.
I think that sounds good.
Bob Dylan said Songs should sound good.

An imagined eulogy. A new connection
made of a cable old and a cable new.
Two cylinders of waxy lip medicine.
I sit here and I ask deeply in my hero-want...
Am I never going to crawl through an air duct?

THE STRANGERS OF THE LAND

We would kill him and leave him for the weathers
but he has the best dreams,
images that direct our wandering
and crystallize our separate nights.
To prove his power
he will say one of our secrets aloud
into the white mist of his breath
but he will never say
whose it is.

He sits outside the light of the fires
and almost everything he dreams comes true
but we keep his neck in a ring of iron
and his body linked to a mule.
He is kept in an old bearhide
and into his wooden bowl
we pour cartilage and yellow broth.
He is a living fit
masturbating and screaming
waving himself in primary frosts
weeping and praying
putting his finger over each star
and winking
in the vast nocturnal clear.

We walk in the cinnamon mud and marigold clay,
around the lavender pools and green alpaca mold.
Terraced mountains and the slow spill
of the glacial ice
that blues and cracks.
Frozen ropes and a brown eagle
that we follow following us.
Our horses with creamfur and sudden hail,
immeasurable white.

On good days we lay ourselves
in the wildflowers of the valley
watching the sky inhale the clouds
watching the branching paths of the rockfaces
the shaking golden tufts

The Ruins

the collected colormoisture
that only twists and vanishes
and there are rockwalls standing in the foothills
like ornamental ash.

He draws in the dirt and we listen as he sleeps,
there he reveals and talks and confides.
Once he said that a healer must wound himself
in order to test his skill.
Sometimes he reads lunulae, and dances a joke.

Our dreams are rigid and calcified,
they are brittle and they break.
They speak in bleeds and rushes and whispers.
Rooms and embarrassments. Childhood bruise.
Their elements warp, they lie, they are only memory.
They are nothing and they are everything,
eating forms to become their own defecation.
They have no purpose, they are sad,
they pitch useless echo and bland repetition.
We turn on the soil and we wait for what he knows.
He,
the low animal of meaning.

He comes upon broken antlers
and he makes a paint of pollen
he knew about the haunted glen
and he healed a lapwing with his tears
he told us about the drought
and he told us about the thieves
he spoke to life the fall of meteorites
and he marked the sick village with his thumb
he knows the stalk of wolves
he knows the sweep of herds
he comes into our minds and begins magical operations
but he tried to rape the young girl
when the girl was still young.

He knew the avalanche, he knows the bad water,
he read the mineral spectrum and he harvested fungi,
he led us through the forever tunnel
and we were born on the other side.

He is intimate with spoor and root
and he deceived the hungry bandits.
Knowledge is a pure script in his body
the future a flowerstem in his hand
and in the moonlight he tries to fly
some believe he can
some have even seen him
but if that is so
why does he stay?

In the petaldrifts of a new spring
he predicted our one child,
the round belly, the dome and fruit,
but we do not know the father.
I have asked and he spit at me and laughed,
threw bones and dandelions and light.
I have come to believe it is him.

YE SHALL RECEIVE

Desperate,
I asked nature to show itself to me,
to give me an opening.
I could not see it.
I could not understand.

I had forgotten my question until yesterday,
and there, among the broad green leaves,
was a branch of red crabclaws.
And when I looked closer
each claw became
a mandible
a mouth
a beak
and within
rows of dirty teeth
arranged like a proto alphabet.

THE EAGLE AND THE SNAKE

Her mouth closed for the long kiss
and the trucks filled with broken trees
went by us
on the street in Roma.

Videos of my dad and sister
singing karaoke at the casino.
A flash of our coordinates
in the rope of infinities
on the plane to San Francisco.
Mom dead two years today.

A man beneath the scar
in the schoolsupply ghetto
near the skysized flag
of Mexico.
There was phosphorescence
and purple minerals
on the white wall
that surrounded her,
a crust of spices
on the halfmoon
orange.

HIGH DRILLING

It's not the noise but waiting for the noise.
Expecting it.

In the foothills there are hounds.
Downtown there are car alarms
and buried music.
High drilling.

Every person is now ominous.
I'm not going to be found
helping anyone.
I will not be targeted.
I will not be misled.
It used to be about beer and music.
Now it's hoping
anyone
anywhere
will love you.

A desperation.
A cold scraping.
It seems no one can hold a plan
anymore.
Click on the golden arrow
to open the flipbook of options.
What emerges is only the man
with the bucket of combs.

WHITE CARPET

The streets were paved with white carpet,
the soldiers careful not to leave polish,
butterscotch on the clouds she drifted
against me, men chucking tiles
in the blue wind. Seven kinds of sickness.
Do you know where she went?
Do you know who she is, talking
what kind of car she'll get
in LA.

In absentia, my sister's friend drugged
in the confetti winds, an old man barefoot
in the flower beds. I used to have a girlfriend
who wanted to walk in the woods, who
wanted to explore, and now what do we want:
entire epochs of want programs. Perfect holes
dug for the saplings on Kachemak Bay,
vanilla glaciers
across the water.

SPIRALBOUND

I remember waitcalendars in pencil
for Christmas, the countdown,
the advent,
figurines of chocolate
and their plastic molds
behind paper doors

and now
the waiting has become
extracted and complete,
ran the contours to become
the object of itself,
jumped the cup
to become the city.

Just one epistle
from a God evermore unseen
could change my parcel of life,
my edict—house at the edge of the development
where a man once solicited (maybe)
a child, my neighbor.

Waiting was a common theme in our songs of boyhood
because the word WAIT
gave us a big A
to sing into RadioShack microphones
(red tinbox of singles and change
for gasoline).
Yes, we all remember the spiralbound atlas.

O we charmed the snake to writhe in its belly.
Redworld of the total bullseye. YouTube treasurebox
of another morose band. Random is for amateurs.
I surpass.

IMPRENTA POP CULTURE

A cyber incident and a fraud alert
(IMPRENTA POP CULTURE: $875.00)
pulsing through the bedsheets
hanging in the windows of CDMX.
Spells, incantations, sunburnt TAROT signs

—blue pylons, plastic,
that keep you from the center
of the center where the president
sleeps on, what I can only assume,
are

pleasant bedsheets.

The waiter obsessed with order...
is she flirting with him?
I wish I could send him a paper crane
whose inner wing states:
I don't care.
Digesting half a pink Adderall,
I'm working on my uppercase Qs
in a personal script.

Mainstream is such a brilliant expression.
I quit the online IQ test.
Whatever, I'm stupid, I said.
There should be outline commas
for the sake of clarity, and not pause.

Oh god the solipsism
of this simulated link-out,
Frida Kahlo's house
in its bold redandblue.
I once tried to follow that scheme
in my first rented room
but only got
the uniform of Spider-Man
and worried friends.
(I settled on rosy salmon.)
I remember I could not sleep
until the room was my degenerate order
of perfection.

The Ruins

STUNTED GLOW OF MACHINES

A place where it is always
amber and orange:
American Thanksgiving.
Stunted glow of machines
and the pride of brick, the level rides
past steam and aluminum
and the bakery cursive.
Taste of dawn coffee.

Long parking lots and the dust in vending machines
and thrift store paperbacks, the
Hondas and Toyotas, the
grit of *The Godfather*. Shadows and mints
at the diner
in the rusted
outdistrict.

She stands between the open windows
and the air new with cold.
You can hear the cars at the station,
a chill descended. She will be so good to you,
bringing cans of beer
and leaving her black hair. Of course
you begin to talk about
God.

A hanged singer in Brooklyn: the Internet the new
communal fire. Bone jaws
lagging behind
their final words. Piles of yellow arroz,
napkins bursting from their mirrorbox.

THE SEASON OF THE HANGINGS

Life is a grand seduction.
Life is a cult perpetuated by a fat crosseyed hermaphrodite
slathered in blood.

And still, when we lose our peers in the season of the hangings,
we rally for life—noisemakers, strong martinis,
our breath reeking again.
Stay Stay Stay
And then we fix the strongest drink there is:
Things will get better.

If it's not malaria or slavery
it's a moneystuffed guru telling us how good we have it.
If we are not punished for our skin
we are fighting off a curious cold.
You will break your own back
trying to convince us
that we're made of rubber.
Billions of dead swarm
in the knowledge you receive
and you will, in the words you inherited,
call it God's plan.
You will do whatever it takes
to push it to the positive.
What are you trying to protect?
You're a lance corporal, at best.

You think people are cynical.
You think they have a naughty attitude.
People are hopeless optimists,
doped on Disney and cinema kisses
and politics and paychecks.
Dreams of unity. Dreams of plenitude.
Dreams of nations. Dreams of gold stacks.
That is why they grieve, that is why they gasp
at the atrocity details, the body numbers,
after all—what is more attractive
than somebody who cares
and gives their eyes to the dew?

That is why there are so many mothers
down the highschool hallway of the ages
shaking their heads, clutching corpses,
clutching pearls, rubbing their knuckles,
counting rosary. But no,
the good life
is merely
a mental adjustment
away.

It is not a condition.
It is exactly what the Greeks called it:
a drama.
Woe the wars, woe the injustice,
sitting in greasy spoons
in the steam of another
séance of grudges,
another ghostdick in your mouth.
Muffled: Someone oughta put this right.

Have you truly fallen for it?
Have the babies made you soft?
Have you gone weepy in history class?
Do you really think there's a coherent plot?
If so, kindly explain it,
through your parents and the village.

Do you really think there are invisible bleachers
and a crowd of the eternally good
rooting for you?
Do you think Time knows how to stop?
Do you think What Is At Hand
gives one good fuck
about the clans and children and gays?
The immigrants. The poor. The rich.
Still, you stammer and spit,
and start to call for the deaths
of a bunch of hooligans.

A smoky room and jaundiced men with a map.
Drunks in the barroom,
listing grievances and getting heated.

You think that's what this is.
Bad intentions. Misdirection.
I know, you're on the side of puppies and natives and cherubs.
You never stop reminding me.
Don't you ever feel ashamed?
Don't you ever feel like a bloated huckster?
Your dumb child is the product of every genocide
and every bell toll
and every guillotine
and every Twizzler
and every balloon
and every slave's prayer.
You shield the offspring from the blood
and give them a nip of whisky,
pat yourself on the back,
and weep when they are crushed
under the wheel.

When someone shows themselves out—
a bullet, a rope, a syringe, a bus—
you get all spooked again,
and you start telling everyone
why life is worth it,
like we're talking
diamondrings and goals.
You unroll the script, you get out the drum,
but you look worse
than any crazy on the street.
You want everyone to stay right here and suffer
(though you never stop hating
the ones you call guilty):
licking sorbet
and making movies
and strumming guitars
and crushing poverty
and knitting quilts
and curing the latest disease,
so you can think of the one you saved
every few months
and remark, "Hmm. Oh yeah.
What a person."

The Ruins

HAPPY AND HONEY

I will spend all my money
happy and honey
on all the beautiful women
in this guttered city.

I will go into the red yolk of love
where the moon shard and white sun lay.
I will tear to Pink Floyd in the echo room
as bachata presses the windows
up from the street.
And I will not look at my feet
in all the dance dens
of these lightdusted neighborhoods.

THE CROW

It's simple really:

I was in a pickup truck in a dream
and I was shot in the stomach
by a man wearing a t-shirt
displaying the melted face
of the woman I love.
The next day

the crow was so black
it was the origin and destination
of the entire world.

I watched it become
the vanishing point
of all time.
And we joked
that the crow
was Ava's boyfriend.

Days later I told Ava
that the crow was on my mind.
My boyfriend?
Yes.
Do you remember that movie *The Crow?*
I do.
So scary. But why?
It's a haunted film.
Brandon Lee was shot in the stomach
on set.

THE WHISPER JUNKIES

When God comes through it will be horselike
Dadlike, like the ceiling like,
spinnbarkeit, albumen,
your dead mother in the walls
you see
when you close your eyes.

You and your stoned friends
run the world,
lint at the bottom
and you can feel it
now
and on that blanket
in Puerto Varas.
The ashman at his computer,
another man
you cannot become.

A SLOWER SMOKE

The green and yellow grass
around the abandoned airplane hangar
has been mown
and this new limit
has allowed it to become
more lush.

Black ants on stone tablets of sky
and the young man practicing age
stands before smoke rings
on the collapsing brick porch,
a worldmap frosted
on his glass mug.

The evening a kind of slower smoke.
On the grey lines of dry bark
the squirrel stiff with fear
will double itself
when it hits the ground.
Rich moss on the faded blocks
and every seam
a future site
of explosive growth.

BLACK INTEGER

I sleep in a small concrete room
that I secured by holding the right skeeball ticket
and beside the bed is a tropical screen.
Gothic palms and a hotpink sunset.
Dogs and frisbees and grinning surfers,
the wallpaint thick and it softens in the real heat.
Occasionally, bored, "warding off regrets,"
I pull the screen down and let it go up,
a miracle of tension and spring.

In the dark space that remains
I see New Orleans after the hurricane.
Streets of glass, X on the house front.
At night the railyard and the red lights
and in the day a helicopter
flying, chained to a vat of water,
toward a black axis of smoke,
a black integer dividing.

I see my old English teacher, and the fantasies therein.
She was flabby and gaptoothed, blonde and smiling.
I was tortured on my bed, twisting, crippled.
Food and her asshole, chewing and kissing,
I was not sure what to dream.

AT THE PEAK

At the peak when your air is broken
and there is a black fire before your eyes
and the world has become white with its givings
there will be a man and his toothpick
a green cap and an old flannel
and he will want to chat as the eagle
circles him.
Malo momento, he will say,
eyes grey and green.

The black dog will come too
leaving no prints on the snow and ice.
Epochs in clean layers, tiers of rock,
the man kicking at the slush
his hands in his pockets,
satellite to an invisible point.
He is not tired and his clothes are unmarked,
you will look and see the shoes are dry
and if he had a small honeycake
a palm of cashews
an urn of tea
a red Duncan yoyo
you know he would share with you,
easy and not cold.

THE CENOTE

In the smiling Brazilian woman
sitting beside the clear Mexican cenote
there are one million dead blooming,
disappearing snakeskin the everpresent
diamondpattern, a more sensuous chainlink,
each unit a mouth, each opening a tunnel
to the tunnel that is always widening god
throwing holes and transfers and I debate
whether or not
to flirt with her again.

The full boredom expression
of the tireless wilderness, wads of paper
with the wasted seed, tropical birds hissing.
Pounding stroking and searching in the halfdark
the quarterdark the fulldark, not dreaming
but witnessing a bluegreen fire of mist,
called up from the deep return to the
league of weeping, to the café districts,
to the long panel of shoppers and the fluttering
prints of dirt arenas, those plastic lids for to-go sodas,
the raised language there, describing a memory
that is remembered now, in the lieu of traffic.

THE REMAINS OF THE BENEFACTOR

The remains of the benefactor
and at the bottom of the well of bones
a pair of black sunglasses.

She took me to the park of fountains.
We ate a plate of meat and potatoes.
We ate donuts covered in syrup.
Spoonfuls of red.
Heated dust.
An actual calloused hand
closed around the heart.

Chapter room and mirror paint.
The lines the crows make
above the palace and the monastery.
Plastic bags filled with white popcorn.
There are always children running
and a vendor arguing with security
and my tinnitus is getting
only worse.

I was with her
but I kept finding another,
our eyes white and meeting.
Her yellow dress and jean jacket.
Decapitated saints and a painted tree
filled with the faces of monks.

Catacombs and organized bone ephemera,
the library of ashen book
and the ticking courtyard,
wood from Central America
and goldleaf and St. Francis:
"He would preach to animals."

I kept seeing her dark eyes
like wandering victories
and she spoke like a Californian.
Her friend hit her head—low threshold
and the guide in his sad lisp:
"Thank you for visiting."

The Ruins

THE TILE CITY

I am waiting for the door
that will lead to the black corridor
between the next door
that will transform me
into a nude baby
slathered in jelly.

Counting céntimos and comparing tax rates.
This year will be the year I become a rock star,
that or a husband or the final mendicant.
Softened cartons around my few goods
and cats I talk to under green comets.

The door to the middle of a waterfall.
The door to the floating powder
and the falling bills and the and the.
A tuffet and a vagina and shadows of future kin.

The door to the séance, the door to the doctor
who shoves a growth in my mouth and pushes me back
back to the night before the reposado glass
back to assorted classics
back to when the bathroom tile was a city.

FOR THE LOVE

A smile that had been to Russia
and she has two dogs she loves
and next she wants to go to India.

A shine to her upper arm
I could not stop watching.
Skin almost reflective,
tanned and tight
around the muscle in form.

A psychologist who works with couples.
A white Audi
and dreams of a big family.
After ten minutes
I abandoned the meal.

I had been arched and working
and trying to get the love.
I have been up on an island
and adrift in the stands.
I have been on the stage
and seated at the desk
working and working and working.

Licking and pressing and arranging documents.
Waiting for the swell
and buying all the drinks.
Balanced photographs of hotel lots
and unique compliments offered
instead of chocolate.

I have danced drunk and danced sane,
tried to learn one million things.
I have relaxed and I have straightened.
I have cultivated rationality
and I have sat on fallen wood
until I began to freeze.
I have painted my face different faces
and broken my throat with attained voices
and made my ears ring

The Ruins

with my own songs
because I did not exist.

Looked into eyes and rehearsed the stories.
Punchlines and poignant lines
and complete absurdity.
Chinese lunch and Peruvian dinner.
Working, always working, even on the shore.

She said it's an American curse.
Spontaneity and control
and unadorned drives
through the vast desert.
Ziplines and bagged drugs
and reinterpreted logic.
Interest and always interesting
and moving toward the sun
and sweating and diving
and not pushing and thereby addressing
but always trying and working.

Beer and the sacraments
and vermouth and O'Keefe.
Working to please, trying to disgust,
failing to appease, and stirring all the dust.
See me working. See me there.

UPON DEATH

I was relaxed
because I was sure I was going to die
and upon death
a number of mysteries
would crack
open and glow.

But then that guy stabbed me
with an eternal-life syringe.

Completely out of nowhere.

HALFTONES

The woman who looked
like an albino monkey
asked her friend
if it was Thursday
but it was Friday.
We were all walking through fog.
I thought a tennisball was going to hit me
but a pole got between us.

I had been worrying hard all day
and then my penis failed me.
I blamed the wine
with the halftone label
that reminded me of the friend
I had dreamed of
the night before.
He could work magic with a photocopier
and taught me how to zoom in,
far deep into the newspaper image,
until the image became
all dots.

WEISGERBER

My only goal in life
is to make women laugh.
It is the highest and lightest honor
of this weeping crippled world.

A Thompson submachine gun
on a long table of reflective walnut.
A cigar. A buñuelo in Medellín
taken with a styrofoam cup
of white coffee and phases.
A spoonful of sugar
will look just like a mountain of it.

I HAVE HAD A CHILD

I have had a child
and I must have that child
behave a certain way.
It will meet my wishes
and my laws and my visions
or it will be punished
punished by my will
by my hands by my words
by my stapled parchments
at the bottom of green hills
by my low testaments
in photovoltaic kitchens.

The child must produce ever ripening fruits of gratitude
in the orchard I dreamed
at a diner in Perth.
Back when I had the blue Honda hatchback.

Confirmation of recent activity,
gravity pulling the filigreed milk
into the reservoir tip.
Complimentary anxiety—
and the [invisible exponent].

In tropical dawns murmured
"I will change."
A thought will generate
lubrication
and a statement will be regretted
for eight solar years
for sixtyfour years of the seasons
before its truth will fall and land
like a gravitational stone fruit
honeyred.

I stared into the crafted milk
of the always becoming pink flowers.
Small marks of white
and then the white varicose veins
on the surface of the sea.

B CELL

I am taking a plane to the conference on climate change.
I am charging my electronics to facilitate the research of entropy.
The elevator clangs and I take it anyway.
Zona segura en casos de sismos.

An unobstructed view of windows and limbs.
I am sensing... four separate building projects.
I have to admit... her hightech watch turned me on.
A generation of searchers vomiting in jungle buckets.

I will step in shit and he will have four daughters with the maid.
He looked toward the pizza oven and said I want a Diner's Club card.
I am falling in love with the silhouette in the crane.
We're going to need a better name for Spanglish.

Among the flying cockroaches there are water vendors.
You will find yourself alone in the bar as the staff does shots
to the song Shots. At some point in life we must SCUBA
or para chute or sail or glide.

Diffuse Large B-Cell Lymphoma.
Everybody getting hungry for more watts.
I am often called a Hater... it's true.
I'm glad you know.
It is best to keep an accurate record and tally
of what we are called.

HEALED AND HEALED

Whenever I set out to die
I was saved and caressed and transported.
Whenever I set out to live
I was insatiable and drunk and tortured
unbearable and mean and arthritic
before I set out
to die again.

Massaged by complimentary mothers
and taken to hallowed ground
where the sheep wander over
the arrangement of stones.
Rescued by an American Indian
in the straw pupil of winter.
Led by a Brazilian stranger
to the bus and to the ferry.
Invited to the party
by a woman who hit me
when she laughed.

God has been so good to me,
has he made me this broken
so I can always receive his love.
Is it a long test of gratitude, of belief,
a rotating ghostprism of perception.
Why has he never turned away from me.
Why. Why does he continue to insist on my goodness.
I live only to curse his world.

Carried by seven cars, one after the other,
and fed warm potatoes in a midnight diner.
Sewn by doctors in screaming rooms.
Healed and Healed and Healed.
Actual blank checks
and a nonsensical job
designed just for me.
Timing beyond perfect,
the clocks all beg to mimic.

There when I indulged

in his variety of bodies.
There when I abstained,
serving gentle mushrooms
and long asphalt.
Supplying guitars, supplying positions,
giving what was needed
even if it was a reason
five years later.

I give mistake after mistake
I have let all the flaws stand
I have obeyed every voice,
losing all signals and becoming all noise.
He has left me to writhe on the bed
only to heat coffee in the morning
and make an introduction
to a woman named Genessis
at the blue laundromat.

PREMONITIONS

He praised me in a dream
and I awoke in the devastation.
I scratched at my neck.
The red dye from the pillowcase
was the cause of the rash.
In the morning I found the white sheets
and the white wall
covered in paprika.

I lay like a great dead king
and she reached out to me in the dark
on New Year's Eve.
I was immoveable, I was beyond,
I could not be touched.
Just like that dream, years ago,
where the woman warrior
with the X of two swords
could not hurt me.

I beat her and laid her in the water,
turtle shells beginning to emerge
as she drifted off
into the cut red sun.
I knew then that I could not go with her.
I knew then that I had lost everything.

On YouTube I heard McKenna say
there are not elements of matter
but elements of time. And J. Doyne Farmer:
the system is deterministic
but does not know what will happen.
Tolstoy laughed
at Napoleon's perceived autonomy
and control. Hitchens said offhand,
we have no choice
but to have free will, and in the midst of déjà vu
Darius finds the dog
he had already seen,
and from here, it looks as if
someone is throwing birds.

IDAHO

What if life really is a test,
a dimension for the arousal of passions.
Its goal is to interest you, to engage you,
to fix you on bodies and races
on national grudges and various terms.

You, with all your minutiae.
Daddy and Mommy
and your big journey.
Pale women trying to get dark.
Dark women trying to get pale.
Who's making money
printing these ancient texts?
I see a man on a rooftop
and I want him to jump.

He called her a year after the breakup
begging for forgiveness.
His life had taken one of those turns
and he needed to lift the curse.

She told me so plain:
I fell in love with the wrong person.
She turned to me and said:
And I'm still in love with him.

On his birthday, my father said he never had a goal.
In a few weeks, he had forgotten we talked.
Habits of selection, patterns of vision.
Most people I've met are content and clean.

Did I escape or did I run away?
Both. Neither. And I will never know.
No one will, but my friend wants me to call her psychic.
$200/hour. Credit card only.

My mother at the dinner table
and a discussion about the draft.
You would serve right?
Her face red, her eyes watching.
I gave my shrug.

The Ruins

She warned me about South American women
and was the only South American woman
to ask me for money: one thousand dollars.
She was trapped in the United States.
Idaho, with two horses.

53

BE KIND TO STRANGERS, BE CRUEL TO FRIENDS

If our lives exist
as a kind of memory
who calls it forward
and who does the remembering
when we cease?

I would rather not get to know you
and I'm not much
past the first impression.
Liking people
is for your twenties
before it all comes to rest
in the expanding ambiguity,
powderblue
and frozen catarata.

The evil
are really just sick.
The good
strike their morning alarm
to be forgotten.
Mothers walk so hard
on thinning soles
to protect their failures
and veterans listen
as assorted births
are regretted.

I hurt you because I know you
and you hurt me because you are now known.
I hurt you, simply, because you are here
and God is not.
Every person
a realized complex.
Every person
a fearmade shape.

It's not severity, no.
It has nothing to do
with right and wrong.

The Ruins

It has nothing to do
with any of that,

it's only ever proximity
and available
cruelty.

ACID IN A RECIPE

My cousin gave me a hit of acid
inside one of his folded recipes.
My uncle would get drunk
and try to punch my cousin.

When my cousin tells a story
it tends to just go, to wander,
like he himself, all over the interstates.
How many summers and how many festivals
and what lineage of drug.
The swirling of color and smoke.
He rambles and drifts
and when nothing seems to arrive
I don't know
who in him I miss.

All too quickly, people just are,
they're not who you thought
they may become
and we love them, because we've learned
the truth about change.
He skis and follows The Dead.
He grills and goes into the desert.
He told me: All you can hope to do
is make peace with your pain
before you die.
He is in and I am outside
but I threw the acid in the garbage.
I kept the recipe.
(But I lost it.)

My uncle is that other drunk,
the one outside the frame of the party,
in a broken house of old toys
with a blackened toilet and no internet.
The last time I saw him he smelled like piss.
He thought it was xmas
but had come on the eve.
We fed him coffee and watched the clock
the one with dust on its rim

The Ruins

until we had to go.
When he still had our future
he crashed a car
and was forced to join the navy.
He got hit by a truck in Florida
and lost his sense of taste
and smell.

My grandma said the drums drove him crazy.
Half acoustic Half electric.
He used to show us washed out videos
of Neil Peart.
I loved him so much
and he was the only one
who told me
to follow my dreams.
Everyone else
seemed to know
the way of dreams.

My grandma begged him to stop drinking
as he stood at the front door
silent and statue
and looked out on the yard.
Other holidays
he would scream from the living room
I wish I was never born.

Feynman didn't drink
so he could protect his brain.
But none of us are Feynman
and we mourn that fact
with malt liquor and tequila.
The film titled π:
my cousin hated the ending
because he did not believe
ignorance is bliss.

I left her because she drank too much
and I left her for the same reason.
Over ten years of messy scenes,
circular arguments,

all those bad theories
whose truth can only be accessed
in the state that wrought them up.
But I was right next to the women
and probably worse,
swallowing and paying and swallowing
until an instinct took me away.

Now, I wish I was very drunk
and not alone. I wish I was screaming
and laughing and kissing.
Alcohol is one of life's only gifts,
for it makes people tolerable.
It makes you speak and care.
No one likes the sober records
and who can actually stand
the moderate ones
the healthy ones?
The juice and the fast.
What is the use
of an average mind, cleared?
Our catastrophes are all we have.
No one wants to know
how dumb and useless they are
without decades of commercial poison.

I do not want to see the line anymore.
I do not want to be held back.
There is nothing to find.
There is no one to save.
Daylight is simple, relentless.
I want to be immersed.
I want to be removed by the activity
by the chemical by the dosage.
I do not want to stand in this unbending street.
I do not want the world to increase its focus.
I want to leap over cars like I used to.
I want the breasts and the asses to find me
to comfort me to feed me.
I want to find the perfect party
and I do not want it to end.

The Ruins

THE WAITING WOMB

The field in its sorting will make appear a semi-doppelgänger.
You if you had prospered. An ideal activated and inserted
Into the waiting womb of the past. So this is who I could have been.
He already exists. As if the echoes crescent backward, ringed vapor.
Solidifying now into the strike of the image and the reset reality.
Stupid and shuffling, sparking match powder out from the curb.
And to leap into the towers of the aluminum crystal, the lysergic cave.
Stalking whatever will change what has already passed.
But it needs to be hammered raw, as in a Tuscan butcher shop
Or the window of a red neon altar of flesh, poultry hanging.

D.R.E.A.M.E.R.

A flash through the room
from the crane in the distance,
a blackandwhite banner on it
rippling.

There are dentists who love their work.
Phones filled with mouths.
And if I were a bigamist
I would definitely go
to Venezuela.

David Lee Roth
and James Woods—
what's the difference?
The old bedroom
and the dawn of train and hunter.

In a dream she texts me
and tells me to come back.
In the morning
I abandon my espresso search
because the call of nature
is too urgent.

We are pathetic
and we are weak.

I thought the word dreamer
then saw D.R.E.A.M.E.R.
on a black t-shirt.
You can live in a bad neighborhood
and not even know it.
If there's an earthquake, she said,
pray.

Jung dreamed of a yogi
who had his own face
and Jung thought,
So he is the one
who is meditating me.

The Ruins

He has a dream,
and I am it.

When I was young
I hated any talk of dreams.
Now it's the only talk
that seems any good.

In Athens Georgia
I stayed in a room
with drums and boarded windows.
No light could touch me, no sound.
I called it The Dream Chamber.

There, I would dream vivid and real
every single night.
It was so reliable, so deep,
that the poles reversed,
and my waking life—

selling my plasma
running through the forest
baking hens
eating BBQ

—became the dream.
It was difficult to say
which world
was primary.
Where does a reflection lie
in the hierarchy
of reality?

And I remembered
my old friend's book of quotes:
The dream is real, and life the simulacrum.

He wrote that in a teenage scrawl
and we hated him for it.
We tried to destroy him,
for originality is to be feared
and eradicated.

THE LAUNDROMAT

When I was a child a man walked into my mind,
over the crest of a hill,
surrounded by the blue of dawn.
I began then to write a story
about an Indian on the plains.
I showed it to my aunt,
a big woman who married a Greek.
The writing was in blue ink.

I was in love with Ms. Deluca,
my teacher in the sixth grade.
A pure and hot and angry love.
She had dark olive skin
and long black hair.
She was stylish and smart.
She was direct and strong.
I stared and stared
and I memorized great historical facts,
pacing in my room,
only to receive her praise,
her transformative alephs.
Alexander The Great
did it by himself.

But I began to see she had an affection
for the athletic kids,
she had a preference for the young chosen,
as all the other girls did,
and I saw it was a force that transcended age.
They joked, they laughed,
her attention kept finding them.
It was not sexual. It was not romantic.
But it was there.

When her father suddenly died,
the man who owned the laundromat,
the entire class signed a card
but I refused. It felt good and powerful.
My absence could make me visible.

The Ruins

Soon after she isolated me after class
to ask me why I had done it
why I had not signed.
I squirmed and I shivered
and of course I did not know.

I hurt her and she was hurt and she said it,
and I saw the tears there,
over the eyes I wanted to touch
over the eyes I wanted to see me.
I was amazed at my silence and cruelty.
I was amazed at my cold resolution.

How could a child hurt an adult, a boy a woman?
How, in all her vision and all her wonder,
how could she not see that I loved her
and that it was only the beginning
of a timeless boredom and friction?
Why, in this afternoon classroom
that has become a golden chamber
between the glass,
did she need me to say it?

THE GOOD LIE

She came from a broken nation
to lie with me on the mattress.
She said, Before everything fell apart,
I used to be a princess.

She didn't like her stepfather
or her father or her father's sons.
She wanted to open a bakery.
She wanted to open a donut shop,
American style.
She had been studying law.
She had been studying karate.
She said I looked like an Israeli soldier.
She said I seemed nice,
which is death for a man
and probably why
I never heard from her again.

We took turns in the shower water.
She slid around me twice.
I kept mistaking the soap for shampoo.
She said that I was strong
and that she liked it.
Who cares if she was telling the truth.
There are those
who know how to tell
the good lie.

SWEET CHILDREN OF ORIGINAL DARKNESS

In the light of a red bulb
in the suburban bedroom
we freebased the trucker speed
and waited for our young hearts
to split and crack
and to become better.

The next day
we drove to the Atlantic
and swam in a storm.
This is what you do when the world cannot kill you.

We ordered pills from the Internet,
and colored dust.
We drank syrups and parental liquor.
We awarded the sinus etherfume.
We smoked the wrong plant
all day long
and eventually
went back to weed.
We crafted paper inventions
and drove under smoldering suns.

Overthecounter treats.
Heavy cans of American beer.
Careful squares of acid called Pyramids
that made the sky fill
with government helicopters.
Fungi and microdots of mescaline.
Horrible dawns, waiting for it to end.
My mother found me alone on the deck,
and I found this memory, my mom now dead,
during an acid trip in Barranco.

An emergency room
where a father looked at me and asked,
What are you kids doing?
Spoonfuls of nutmeg
and those pills Giovanni had...
I still don't know what they were.

DMT as Chopin played
in the tasteful Brooklyn living room.
Random burning mounds
of molly,
your fingertip
dipped in crystal.
Then the desert of tequila
and waking up
in the middle of your own
screaming monologue,
in the middle of a life
you no longer understand
(even more).

Blue bags of bad cocaine.
Mexican beer now
and more mushrooms
with long white stems
to enter the dimension
where the specters and images
rise from the bottom
of the inner lake.
"Man is a gateway."

Sugar and caffeine
and a long rainbow of oils.
Black & Milds and American Spirits.
I see now again
over the window
every smooth flame
I have ever witnessed.

Those terrible pints of Georgi
and wailing in New York City.
The liquor store clerk
who told me to stop drinking.
Eating and eating
to absorb the waved puddle
and the ten thousand regrets.

The Ruins

The blue bowl purchased at Warped Tour
and masturbating high,
how sharp and vivid the women were.
Finding the stashes of perfect darkness
in the old Christian town
to get stoned and to walk stoned.
Have we done too much
or not enough?

When I listen to rich Nebraskan men
I am glad to be
messy and superstitious.
"Sweet children of original darkness,"
we were born sensitive and loving
we wanted softness and curved motion
but we were all struck
for clinging to paradise
each in our own way
each at our own time
and we killed what needed to be killed
and hurt as we had been hurt.
We began to amass and we began to cut.
We were material and substance
and we treated ourselves as such.
Each a healer.
Each a destroyer.

Though in this cold Lima morning
and in the solitude of this path
I can feel him flicker and turn
in the unmarked earth:

the one
who has always been able
to wince.

MADE SMALL

I remember my grandmother on the armchair throne.
She made everyone small
she pointed at your belly
she scratched at your mole
she worked at Pizza Hut for fun.
In the coloring book
she told me to outline in black
and color in one direction.

The Germans could be harsh
and to grow you had to take it
until you could give it.
And now I think of these recent years
where I am always looking for a good chair
to sit and dispense, to criticize and to mock,
to break the boredom with the truth.

Or I avoid the chair,
I get dizzy and evasive, I get winded,
I disappear and I insult myself
because I do not want to take it up,
I do not want to say it,
because I know the room hates the one who does:
I do not want the countenances to fall.

But if I stay here circling
the words will find me,
what we all know and what we all
hide from,
so I choose the coward, the distance,
I take off, I scatter, I apologize,
I would rather be made small again.
I do not want the countenances to fall.

We used to pick red berries
and she told me to stay away
from the septic tank.
She said she hated whole wheat
because it reminded her
of famine.

The Ruins

LET US NOW BEGIN THE PROCESS

Let us now begin the process of examining our myriad failings.
You are a drunk and I am a coward.
And both ways and our communication is a sad prince
kicking wildflowers down the stone hallway
of blurred portraits and massacred plates of olives and cheese.
You love your swells of technology more than you love any person.

I am remote, among the stars I cannot name, making the same meal
for this decade and the next, the potential décor sprouting fur.
Unexplained, hesitant, touching young versions
at a table motionless, in a shifting storm of kitchens.

Hint and dream and a shimmering warehouse.
You cough up a compliment when you feel threatened with anonymity,
all the men running from you and toward you and now I am one of them.
Still can't make it past Leviticus, still can't name African sections,
marveling at pathetic encouragements from the one they call God.
A collector of navels.

Observant of what I choose to observe: windswept trash
with all the other grey-eyed kings of the shortcuts
lounging in dens, eating ovencooked cheese pockets, high on cheap opium.
Compact discs instructed us how to be so we can never undo the damage,
paying frazzled men and women, buying the hype and latenight pop.
Memorizing card numbers, memorizing track listings,
trying to encircle that moment when the idiocy was justified.

Botched tattoos, you're so cloying for a pat any claw will do.
But you shake it and present a joke, like me, glowy and obvious with loss.
Food, we love food, an anomaly very human. You are still young
and maintain a definite charm, while I darken and obsess
in an aloof ghetto, populated by myself.
I keep moving out and moving in, nodding in triumph.

I will have sex with anyone in a blank room and you like waterfalls.
I like a schedule so white the paper begins to flame
and you must put a word in everyone's mouth.
If I were to float and leave the ground I would maybe be happy
and on the mattress you vibrate with dreams of soap and gala.

You were born so lucky you come into a new shoe with every step,
you pay and you get 200% back,
and when you smile and return it you get the sum squared.
You're all tan skin and quaking breasts, you laugh and the cynics turn.
You could not be more in it, you are singing and grinning,
and I am swirling draft beer in the bathroom aromas.

We were too much alike and now we are too different.
We had two lifetimes to speak but now we watch movies
so lifelike we squirm in our beds, mouthing No at the stupidity.
And I have not grown into anyone,
have not achieved any desired state,
only let it go unbroken:
a bad habit of meeting people.

THE SEVEN YEARS

Seven years are gone
but you learned just yesterday
what the ancients put to song:
nothing has changed.
Sure, your mother's dead.
That's a given, and you're not surprised.
You knew it when she was weeping
over the phone
about the death of the last cat,
the one you named
as a child.

The family had become
politically divided
all heated and rash at xmas dinner
and her children
were alone in foreign rooms
trying to get as far away
as the limited globe
would allow.
The cheap wine
was getting easier and easier to drink
and the Vantage cigarettes
were quit too late.
Did anyone even care
that her foot was beginning to swell
that she had put on an old cat's worth
of weight?

And you still prefer to run and ruin,
it is how you make yourself felt:
through sudden disappearance.
A cheap trick, amusing maybe once,
but now the only trick you know,
a messy clamoring
for more freedom
in the dirty shadow
of a highschool vending machine.

Bad feelings
because things end badly

because they never end
as the true end
is only theoretical
and that is the glorious day
your own heart stops.
And after seven years
you're beginning to suspect
that everyone succeeds
at your expense.

We don't stay off the fault lines by the way,
we build civilizations on them.
And in seven years
there have been a few babies
a few suicides
a few abortions
a few heated elections.
But as usual, the good news
is disputed
along with the bad.
Though the couples
are just as miserable
and the teenagers
are just as angry.
Have the prices gone up?
because it's officially funny now:
no one can afford anything.

You've meditated
only to become more distant and strange.
You've eaten
to disapprove of the suction.
You've loved
only to fear pregnancy.
You've drunk quite heavily
to turn yourself as joyful
as everyone appears to be
at the crackerjack death rave
in the stripmall down the way.

Your aunt told you
that she was proud of you

that you were in control of your life
right before you panicked
in an alcohol-induced stun
and bought a random ticket to Peru
proving to a few people
that strangers
should not be trusted.

In seven years
it has become scientific fact:
people only love dogs and cats.
They cannot be bothered
with these maniacal apes
who praise themselves
and kill themselves
who collect animals
to keep their neighboring apes
crazy, cycling, and awake.

Seven years of increasing selfies.
Seven years of passive aggression.
Seven years of voluntary fleecing
turning my pockets out
to the self-dubbed witch
and star reader
to the moviemaker
and the owner of rooms.
Seven years of
I'm an erotic puzzle
I'm a Rubik's cube
I'm a complicated light show.
The back of the hand
goes to the forehead
in our bar dramas
in our statehouse shootouts
as the great crosseyed hermaphrodite
huge and selfpregnant
continues to masturbate
with its dead siamese twins
three of your fingers
in the sand of its mouth.

STOP APPEARING

Excelsior and melatonin, Airbnb support
and gangsters rating the accuracy of movies.
My sister made it out of Rio—sudden blue
and white churches, like the Greek flag.
You can buy purple pasta.
You can buy headphones that instantly break.

The trees look upside down, the women talk
on either side of the fried goods. Slow couch
sitting in the barbershop alight with skateboard
stickers, a smiling woman in the dry doorway
and a child beyond, in the lines of the tiles.

The fan pushes on the boas. Stop appearing
out on the street, out in the blackdirt fields,
stop, candles in a spiral, wicks like rope.
Corrugated, terracotta, I want a thread through
the jungle, and they will hide the correct tollfree
number. Stop asking. Stop returning.

Dads, apartments with hammocks, saws working
in the blade mornings, a tall cousin who is still in love,
we chased a cry in the night but it was a mountain fox,
dream of the mechanical headdress, and the rifle suicide
of the chief commander, eyes becoming green feline
to show death is nothing.

THE INHERITANCE

You will awaken from another man's sleep
in a neighborhood of car alarms and busses.
And as you take your jeans
from the floor of the house,
the museum of a newly forgotten house,
you know that you have inherited
the anxieties and terrors of the man,
and all of his mistakes.

You do not know why your nail is black
and there are all kinds of disappointed people
making the phone glow.
You are haunted by momentum
from the steps you never took
from the decisions you never made
but are now yours.

The source is not yours
but the sadness is
as the neighbors begin to wake
as the bodies make their demands.
A bottle of sealing wax
knots of wires
exposed doorbells
and the smell of dampness.

Your memories have fused with his
to make a world familiar and slightly doubled,
unbearable and silly,
with an empty seat next to you
on every plane.
You've been here before
in this place you've never been,
and the language spoken
is almost yours, the question now ringing,
la pregunta de mi vida:
How many abandonments
will it take
to find the man who caused
my enduring innocence?

Frequency and vibration,
the echoes of the nights
where the water decides to drip,
apologies halfwritten
to people full gone,
and burn winds
from future disasters
heat the room
and turn it bright
before its normalcy
hardens into
a grim cast.

Hatred goes long
and so much money is missing
and the people who do remember you
remember only your fear.
Empires entropic
and the timelines prove it.
Simply no one to complain at.
Dust and mold and wreckage,
skin aberrations and cutlery,
bills actions scenes truths,
seven rolls of papertowels,
sparking outlets,
none of which
bear any resemblance
to who you think you are,

but as you limp down one of the roads
you see the mist of the ocean
where people sculpt themselves
and try to forget their fathers.
The foam like cream.
The cliffs like chocolate.
There are hummingbirds in the trees
and the flowers must be prototypes.

And as the 24hour people
of the convenience store
scowl at you, curse you,

The Ruins

you begin to wonder
if the man should be pitied
forgiven
praised.

THE LAST BALLROOM

When we meet again it will be in the last ballroom
and there will be cold cranberry juice
to slake the thirst we had
all of our lives
without knowing it.
And our kiss
will be the kiss that eluded us
when we tried to turn the grey
of the city
into blue.
Your hair will obey you there
your love handles
and we will joke
like only we can
and before the plush hotel room
with a view of the sea
there is a migration of cold sushi
and maybe I will even
apologize.

You I will meet in the alpine cabin,
a refugio in Patagonia,
above the emerald waters.
Straw on the floorboards
and cold bottles of beer
and hot coffee
in blue metal cups.
Charcuterie, wild flower,
an air that sex breathes
on the ancient regal bed.
For breakfast, blue robin eggs,
red bacon, fresh goat yogurt
and granola, not too sweet.

You, an old Mercedes in the desert,
and you, a big apartment
in New York City.
When we finally leave
the stained white cloth
we find long streets of autumn

The Ruins

and the steamed windows
of the ramen shop.
You moan and blink
slow as you eat
and we do not talk
as I squeeze your thigh.

And you, of course,
our own beach
with the sand you like
and endless caipirinhas
or maybe a dark bar
in a secret hotel
with cold and dirty
gin martinis
up.

IN THE CLOSING OF EACH WINDOW

I used to rub her cheek, affectionately,
until I began to notice
a darkening
where my thumb would work
and it was then I noticed
it was not her skin
but some total fabric,
an allskin,
and below that
came the quadrille lines
the necessary vacuum
my own eye.

The footage of the volcano will segue to the beach furniture commercial.
The kidnappers will tell the woman to get better security at her job.
The brother of the star will drink himself to death.
The smartphone will not catch,
the toilet will not flush.

And how embarrassing
to meet our own waste
to realize we have pissed out
another two months
in our sleep,
clutching lottery tickets.
Even in our dreams
we crush our thumbs
in the closing of each window.

She will leave the apartment as the church bells start to ring.
The bowling alley massacre will elicit a chuckle or two.
The computer will become a perfect friend.
The money will not come,
the lock it will not lock.

Perhaps those who say
"I don't believe in love"
are those who have been
infused with love.
Perhaps the fortunate

and the fed
can afford to be cynical.
But when the coin grows bored
(the obol, the danake)
and finds a new pocket
the owner will know
hope
is just another
propaganda.

BRAZILIAN SOAP OPERA

The thieves had to admit that the hardest part was choosing the masks
and when I awaken my eyes are tired from tracking the dream.
My father sends photos of the gravestone with red roses
and the Internet is afire with the wasted life of a ghostwoman.

The last time she smoked she noticed the orange flowers of the patio
and put her fourth stub on the stainless steel.
The aunt with Down Syndrome died at 50 of natural causes
and my cousin with MS... We haven't spoken in a while.

Her mother asked her why she would ever want a bicycle, as it would just be stolen.
He will wait until the summer to see where his girlfriend gets a job.
Every time we meet she complains about the same alcoholic
and what a blessing to be lost at the supermarket.

Last night at the gas station they were giving away plastic cups of beer.
Last night at the gas station I watched five minutes of a Brazilian soap opera.
The distorted teenager will follow his mother with the oxygen tank
and the movie will be ruined by flashbacks and music.

The imperial cats are loved more than the flawed and running parents
and the last time I saw Randon he talked about Grandma's bargain chandelier.
I invited him to my old boss's apartment but he chose to sleep in the truck
under the bridge with Crystal and their coolers and grill.

To whom I've attached an onionskin of grievance he has finally gone solo.
And the Braveheart obsessive is now a star,
father's shotgun no longer in his mouth.
I drop his name as fast as I can to the guy who dresses in purple
and ultimately matches the rollgate by the bar.

If one eats too many cubes of fried provolone one will become sick.
She was drinking quite a bit of wine there there at the end.
I know the couple are now engaged but I won't say anything.
I was calling him tío and had forgotten he was an uncle.

The homeless man has laid himself facedown upon the grate
and he has fixed a small blue cloth to his back
and when the subterranean winds blow he is a man falling through the air,
hopeless, amusing all who pass.

The Ruins

THE ROSE GRADIENT

I don't touch the landscape anymore
for fear of making
an accidental purchase
or letting loose
my important numbers
my 4D columns
of information.

She threw rice and white petals
at her son's wedding
and the next day
she needed a lung transplant.
There are those claiming
the American Empire
is at an end.

The man wearing a Santa hat
yells at the twin dogs
standing on the cart he pulls,
guarding his burial mound
of cardboard and rope.

Threat streams and ultramarine...
Forced multiplier
and the municipal cemetery...
The heat is leaving the hot water
so you'd better send a valentine to someone.

Do the new strange sounds
that find you in the night
tell you something
of your own death
the one approaching
beside the apocalypse.
And why shouldn't they be
two heads
in that infinity symbol
stockade...
A double yolk.
Siamese twins.

Maybe the global
should be read as the personal.

What sounds like a cane
striking the cement
moves down the avenue
and a helicopter is sent
to vibrate the roofs
and disturb the pigeons
that are beginning to take up a language
somewhere in the rose gradient
of the window.

A SMALL GOLDEN GEAR

A small golden gear
on the tip of your tongue.
A night of nightmares,
with a trolley track laid down upon
the rimworld of the poor,
the garbage-strewn retina,
with the boys throwing green bottles
at the sordid lacerations.
Orange latenight stores
like controlled cubic burns.

I finally walked naked
in front of the ceiling camera
to look on the glowing backyard
to see if the fated thief
had finally arrived,
as Noela rested
sealed and opulent.

In the morning
the birthday balloons
are still mostly inflated and
we both have stomachaches.
In the night
in the barrier between
the true and the true
a beast
nibbled at my toes,
a bleached woman
lived secretly
in one of the many rooms
of the permanent dreamhouse,
and there was confusion
and discrepancies
and my old friend
in religious garb.

So now the whole day
is gritty with the residue
of nightmare, of neglected things,

of data shards, of menace, and
I must wait
for a soothing image
a positive remark
a flying dream
to clean and wash
to leave a calm wave of soap
on the many lenses.

EVERY TREE

Every tree
is an advanced building
from a prior race
is part of a living
parallel race
is a future race
and we must eat of the trees
to speak with them
so that we too
can become
our perfect buildings.

Intimations of death
all the long while.
Young coconut flesh
on the cool white sand
and the patient surfers
past the arrival
of most of the water.
That woman is famous
but I missed her.

The source of the beeping
that takes tropical birds
out of the sky
is soon revealed: the rising
of the parking garage gate,
white and steady.

Everything must now
insist on its being, all of us running
from the dementia
growing spherelike
in the placeless place
behind our eyes, behind
even that.

Language rises
from the empty core
to meet its true execution

in the city, as if
it made the conditions
for its own dominance, shaping
mind and the world inside it
to better flourish.
In the city
you reach for the word,
in the forest
you wait for the image.

Mute in its transcendence
verdure catalogues our folly
and speaks
in a remembered drone,
before burning
in our periodic fires.
And we ask together,
Do we commune
with what we will become
with what we were
with what we are?

The Ruins

LESSER SHAPES

The shiatsu therapist
told me to stop playing the victim.
Women are always telling you things,
pointing to the future,
out where the sun appears,
while men
secretly hope for your death
so there will be one less man
at the vertical ribs
under that same sun
merciless in its breeding
of conniving
lesser shapes.

THORNCROWNED

We are never where we want to be
and that is the sum of it,
though much graphite is shed
in the drawing of it.

The roots hang like dry hair,
the taxis have lost their monopoly,
and greed is a long secret word
we hear in our dreams
but do not remember
though we awaken
itchy and different.

There should be better laundry
to hang
and the foot should be shaped
by a leather more fine
even though our troubles become colored sand
persecuted by wind
on the stone floor
in someone else's memory.

She said they would know I was decent
at the passport control.
My sister mastered my mother's pignoli recipe
in one or two tries.
We have my grandmother's baptism certificate
and we are looking forward
to Italian citizenship.

We are after
different light
in the mountains, glade, and courtyard,
dark eyes opening above flowered pillows,
numbers that embarrass us,
we want a broad freedom
to fix and tap our mistakes.
The painter's father
also has a studio.

The Ruins

Catapulted
to let rooms
where a bust of thorncrowned Jesus
is silhouetted
by a square of frost.

THE AGE OF MANUAL DEXTERITY

Confetti at the prosthetic center
and charcoal hoses at the gas station
in the long season
of the bedroom hangings.

A fallen urine cloud
between the city and the hills,
and the plastic lid
does not fit
the paper coffeecup.

Foraging in the bad layouts
of eight million websites,
assaulted by deals
but we are thankful for it
when we think of a candy bar
in the hot stream
of a good shower
when she released herself
into the palm of your hand.

The white curtains turn
on a Mediterranean terrace
and we are
exact in our crimes
because there is nothing better
than getting away
with anything.

In the age of manual dexterity
and lithe finger
and rainbow trail left by eager arc
people are easier and easier
to delete
but maybe
harder
since there is more evidence of them.
Whereas they used to be
a colorful swathe
on a khaki map

that would become more inaccurate
with time.

I warned her
not to give the boy
too much thought
not to treat him as a problem
with an answer
and I still think it good advice
with the sweat going cold
on my back
and I asked out the receptionist
at the dermatologist office
but she said no, she gets out too late.
Only minutes earlier
she almost sat on my lap
to help me with the emblematic city
of the Greek paperwork.

THE SUPRAPATH

Have you noticed that you knew the dead man
who played bass on the album
you are now using to console yourself
about the loss of a woman
from the city
whose name sounds like the name of the woman
who you thought was your final and ultimate love
who told you about that house
where you hear your love before you meet them
and get sick
as they wander the barren rooms
of your life.

And have you noticed that as the confusion of your life reigns
as darkness leads to darkness
as the jokes get better
but harder to laugh at
there is now a hurricane decimating some coast
and it has your name
and the aerial photograph of the calm white destroyer
reminds you of a drawing you made
years ago
based on an image that has been with you
since the beginning of memory.

And have you noticed that all this is happening
in the land your dead uncle was from
where tomorrow you will go to see the ruins
and think of him and his generosity
and how he once described
your young but now ongoing predicament
with one word:
Confusion.

Did you notice that you kept seeing 9:11
on your phone
the weeks before your mother died?
And that your sister, over a year later,
told you that your mother had come to her
in a hyper-real dream

and she was young and beautiful
in a white room
and she told your sister it was going to be okay
but she has not visited you.

Did you notice your name
followed by two exclamation marks
on the wall in Heraklion,
and that one mosquito
always seems to ruin
the deepest meditation,
and that the friend
who called his dad an asshole
when asked to mow the lawn
is now a farmer,
and when you first arrived at the farm
that friend was mowing the lawn
and his dad had broken
the previous machine.

Did you notice the woman
who could not stop pulling out her hair
has become a celebrated hair stylist
and that your young grandmother
looked like a young Bob Dylan
and told you that you were good at writing lyrics
and that hair stylist told you
There are only like nine faces.

And have you forgotten
that your father had a comicbook shop
in the haunted Farmer's Hotel
and that years later
you would hear the song
"The Farmer's Hotel"
by Silver Jews
about that same haunted place
but think it nothing special
until years later
when you had come to their music
while working at a pie shop
and "Sleeping Is The Only Love"
became your favorite song.

Have you noticed that the hopeless boys you knew
are now fathers and tattoo artists and women
and that people have built their lives
out of broken tile and spilled potting dirt
and that one guy
who used to drive with the tall bong
fell in love in Guam
and once stole a bike
to escape a coming tidal wave.

And what about that most generous woman
who lays out pictures of the dead and orange petals
and shots of tequila,
how her sister and her wife were struck down
but she still arrives every morning
with the handcart
and meat and blood in a bag
and boxes of ripe avocado
and she hands to the illegal immigrants
and the hungover citizens
timecards and cash
fixed together
by a paperclip.

And why have the women been so kind to you?
And why did JG Ballard name that book
The Kindness of Women?
But why was your first hatred
born through a woman named Geard
the duplicitous babysitter
long ago
in the time of Clinton and Bush
when the world was populated with crazed adults
and now you are one of them
angry at children for continuing to appear
in a life that is more of a prison
like Céline said
though I haven't been able to find the quote
for about seven years.

The Ruins

Did you notice that your baby cousin was preyed upon
by some irreversible
demyelinating
disease
and now reads science fiction
in the county of your youth
but that his halfsister
your stepcousin
was once described as
"the nakedest person in TV history,"
and that her mother
said she wanted to read
The Tibetan Book of the Dead
where you found the lines
"When I roam the life cycle driven by strong instincts,
May the Hero Scientists lead me on the path
Of the clear light of orgasmic wisdom!"

And remember when the native
actually gave you sagelike advice
the day after Thanksgiving
and drove you off the reservation
where you were looking for death,
and the UX designer
in Santiago
told you
that you will not find death by looking for it,
and when she came
it sounded like she was being murdered.

And the man
by the Bagmati River
where the sugar and the bodies burn
told you to never look a monkey
in the eye.
And shortly after you left
that very ground was remade
by the restless turning
and the nervous sleep
of the many layers
of the earth.

FROM MEDELLÍN TO NEW YORK

She held the dog up to the phone
and it was a puppet
and then a dog
and then a puppet again.
Say hello, Gigi!
I'm confused, I said,
is it a real dog or not?

She had gone to New York City for work.
But I wanted her to stay in Colombia
so she could begin to tend the garden of our future.
I didn't tell her that.

A guy once told me,
I like you, you're always the same.
Then he said he wouldn't fuck me
but he would love to fuck my clone.
I find gay men
give the best compliments.

THE EMBASSIES

The black ants had stopped moving
on the yellow slice of peach
and all the embassies were shuttered—
Moldova, the Sudan, the Congo—
and a man twirled a tail of leather
around his fist
as girls danced in the arid yellow of the hall
in the Athens twilight.

The cute woman
who works at the 24hour spot
said she was excited to be going to work.
She got a creamy iced coffee,
her white headphone wire twisted,
and sat at a table in the shade
to kill the remaining hour.
I like my job.

THE HOUSE OF TOO MANY SWITCHES

Most things aren't true,
but there is a suncooked blonde who sits behind the desk
of the rentacar place down the road,
and behind him is a blued recreation of Greek ruins,
and he is dating the woman sitting there
with silver eyes—
the poet from Russia.
She stood and left
when the men began to joke.

Today a man came into the building
and straight to my neighbor's door.
He was selling bananas,
screaming out the Greek word for bananas.
I heard it through the door:
my neighbor didn't have any money
but her husband had some.
The man asked where the husband was
and then the husband was there, out of breath.
He had been across the street, at the small church.

It took me too long to realize the man could have been a thief
or worse.
I saw him walk down the road, screaming the word again,
but with no vigor and he entered no house.
White shirt and black sunglasses and a plastic bag with bananas.
Have you seen him?

The trees have been pushed by the wind
and they lean all around that church,
crowding the little yellow house of god
with the pale blue trim.

And on the autumn sand the people look dead,
and no one knows the house I saw
with the long staircase to the private beach.
Tonight I will sleep with the blue Veltihome knife.

The Ruins

HOW CLEAN THE DOWERY

Lavender
she held
and how clean the dowery
and how glad the man who took me through the orange petals
and how black and cubic the drone that filmed us.

How is the village where the animal is butchered
in the heart of the town of shifting paths
where on the shadow side of the mountain like a silent stranger
there are men crouched before a dot matrix of blood.

Circles on the floor of the clay house
where the wind lifts the sand and the dust
and the edges of the browned napkins
the center pressed by a deck of cards.

There are black veins of water on the floor,
can you see?
And in the stirring we do things to them.

OVER THE FACE OF THE WORLD

Several different points of water,
and a red BMW.
A white crucifix standing against the storm clouds,
and a man screaming at a woman at the terminal gate.

When Mom was dying the vomit would pour
like a waterfall of sewage
down the clean soft fabric the nurses would replace.
And in DuoLingo Spanish
the last lesson is the conditional perfect.

The Italian doctor was worried about the brown spots
on my lips
and told me not to worry
about the white spots.
We don't investigate ourselves, he said,
meaning don't be scared by everything you notice.

We are good to our various containers
or bad,
it doesn't really matter.
There is a randomness to it
that will not be so random
when we are through the randomness
that gave us what we feared
and what we were expecting
and perhaps what we engineered
in the toxins we befriended
in the sins we committed
in the dreams we coaxed into being.

Plato waits for us on the perfect plane
on a fainting couch with a nest of grapes.
White marble with smoke veins
and mineral impurities.
But for now we are listening
to the manual vacuum over hard carpet
and the struggles of children
in foreign stairwells.
There is paperwork,

there are numbers on the screen,
there is that one traffic light near the home
that takes longer than all the others
all the others over the face of the world.

THE TOTAL FIELD

When each ant on the back of your desert eyelid
is an entire people wandering and lost
This is the total field

When you see your purple hand against the ceiling
and it waves to you as you know
it was the wallpaper flap of healing
seen days before in a dream
you will know that you are in
The total field

When the empty water bottle on the fridge
is the godhead shining blue,
partially obscured,
and you look to your left
to see the modem light
as the blue dawn
This is the total field

When your ancient brothers
are trying to get you to jump
from the fifteenthfloor balcony
because you forgot how to fly
This is the total field

When you are hiding in the prison realm you built
because you grew bored with your own power,
banished from yourself, asleep to yourself
This is the total field

When you cannot escape the burning air
and the world you create begs
for your ingenuity and your mercy
You have found yourself again, locked in the total field

When you know the grain and substance of the one
When you know the geometry and knowledge
of the vehicular human body (archive and weapon)
When every hint and clue
be it film or book or person or memory or idea

The Ruins

is now a direct and complete voice
is now a vast indivisible teacher
You are hearing the total field

When you weep and sing and drool and smear water
with your long lost generations
around a coffeetable in Lima
on the steppe in the lucid night
When you partake of the smoke breath
and give birth to the blue sun
When you give birth to yourself
and awaken as a great warrior giant
When you are the maker and the made
and the wind beyond the poles
When you are Noah under the stars
and the bed is a lullaby ark
When you contact your dead mother
and her presence overwhelms you
because you remember peanut butter
on a burnt English muffin
When you are the eternal monk
walking the rope of infinities
When the intelligent light flows
finally correct
and you are turning and angling
in the right dance
to the music you make
on the cheap plastic floor
When you traverse the unified bloodwork
and tremble in the singular memory
When you writhe and hum
under the seductive and logical possession
of the violet serpentine spirit
When one hand is light
and one hand is dark
and they run each other in harmonious friction
When you are going to return to Paradise
and you are already there
When there is no one to talk to
and there is nothing left to explain
because you have finally gone crazy
it will be you and me
It will be you and me The Total Field

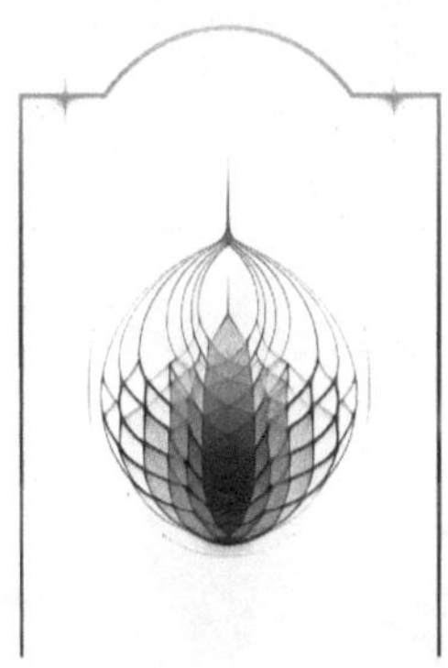

Book 1
Turn the page.

Book 2
Page 249

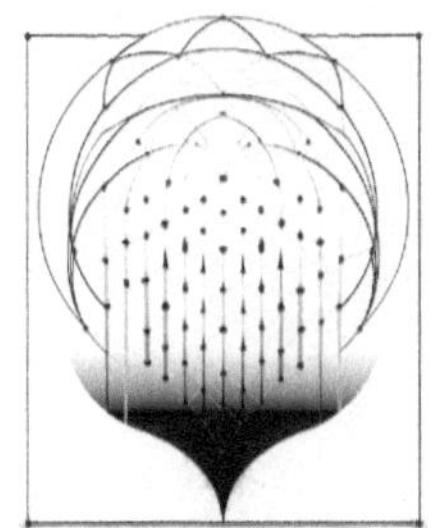

Book 3
Page 333

The Fires

Book 1
The Past, Fire
Initiates: The Path of Transmutation
Centers: Olinda, Goshen
Threshold: Sacred Fear

THE FIRST

DOUBLE MILLENNIA COFFIN

When the heavens are alight in their chambers
and the organ player smashes his face against the keys
and great silks sway over the pad where we lay
there are night dogs aligned on the top of the hill
and comets are pitched green embers in wild arcs
and the dead mingle with the smoke and perfume of the incense.

Gold and jade were found in the double millennia coffin.
The aliens are competing through their abduction and spook programs.
They have come from the supermassive compact object at the center of our universe,
which is the pupil of a stone well in the fourth recurrent dream of the coma body.

THE FLYING LADDER

Reach forward in the dark to provoke the other prisoner
into numbering the dimensions of the prison
and any possible escape beside the obvious levitation.
Total light inhale or is this blindness,
in the vision remainder there is still pink latticework,
there is still bioluminescence, maybe we too
can make our skeletons powerblue.

Where the stupas rebuild themselves
with astonishing infamy, with flying ladders,
with circumspect and paperthin spheres,
the whitehaired woman pulling apart threads of the south wind.
Amassing collateral damage in burntorange dawn,
in the clatter of haunted hotels roamed
by a plainspoken mother, by devoted staff,
cold water for the invisible leprosy,
for the disease thoughts like rainbowed computer tape.

Chasing disembodied shadows on the high field,
the stone stairs reach throttled trees, baseless mountain range,
fog spectra in irradiated pathos, wooden rooms a balm sector-end.

THE LATEST STRAIN OF THE BLOODFRUIT

The interior of the tortoiseshell that is the roof of your mouth
—you will touch the light of the expectant user.
Conferred and transferred to harmonious elevations
by the crimson paragraph
by busstop literature
by the failed caricatures of your father
scratched into the opaque glass.

Humbled in the windstations of the grid.
The bloodfruit has been pulverized and drawn into the city pipes,
the reflection of the blinking red light in the meadowland water
has hardened into the latest strain of the fruit.

Coalesced in airport memories.
Crushed and mimeographed by iron age machines lubricated with kiwi oil.
Laughter a spoiled air, a distressed humming embryo of pure static.
You are crouched and dispossessed below sports television,
cucumber slices on black discs of leaked moisture summon
the image of a pile of school chairs.
This means the abscess has finally arrived on your
most believable mask,
the one that distorts its reflection
through an ancient configuration of microplastics,
which have been found in the placentas of
unborn babies.

THE TOMB OF DANIEL

The tomb of Daniel and the lush names of liqueurs.
He is circled by the lions of straw and bitter orange
and our faces are reddened in the cherrylight
of Grand Marnier. I stumble into the cold room
where the minor prophets are embalmed
in Cointreau and citric rind, in roasted garlic and thyme.

The exposed roots are fingerbones, knuckles,
and white flamingos stand in the rows of the strawberry farm.
Four drops of raw milk fall into the teacup of clean blood
and when you open your eyes in the Mayan morning
you must first remove the calm lids of honey.

We are softly enchanting the clouds as we roam in white robes
but our robes are black in the rich hum of the pink horizon.
I kiss you and push my tongue through the agave and spice,
through your nested tombs, through your complacent ages,
through the liminal decoration of iridescent wreaths
through the outerborough taverns of amber
into the garland your tongue almost makes
and the algae is an electricity of lime.
We become slow, we become peace mongers,
slow drifting in syrup clear and hourmelt,
your long lashes against my lashes
and we are kept and apricot in the arachnid ropelight.

ETHEREAL VIPERTRACE

Ethereal vipertrace in the symmetrical coral
but the street trucks have returned
with their instructional memory
in the permanent dawn of oxygen hiss.
There are pistons in the flora if you wait long enough.
If you let your vision disfigure into the alchemic void of regular magic.

My grandfather, haired again, will tell us the miraculous
story of his life, but first he must have an enema.
A mysterious fourth in the resulting car ride.
Father sister it and I
through the strip of bluescape.
Adherent to dogmatics in nasal parlor tricks.
Seeing through the reflections to see the eye.
Past deliberate madness, past obscure numberfall.
Alphabetized progrock cassettes and needlepoint haybales
are the main arbiters of my categorical readings.
Forgive my vanishing. Forgive me this huge embarrassing tip.
I will need your support in the trial of embers and recall.

THE TWO DREAMS

She dreamed of me sick and sweating
after she dreamed of us having sex.
I said Maybe I'm dying.
Do not even say that.
We're human.
You still have to give me babies.

The sun is diluted silver.
It is rising and descending.
It is following a lateral arc.
The bullet is dinercream white.
The puddle is royal green.
The birds are flying backward.
The birds are frontward flying.
The rhetoric is fakakta.
Her throat is serene.

Black incisors and the threedimensional fingerprint,
the fingerprint in hard honey.
A mouthful of dimes and the Texan supercell.
Already vanished, already forgotten,
volley and ricochet in productions
of the Highway Dept.,
the rime ice of screenwork.

Another friend had also dreamed of me.
The same night. Told the same day.
I was wearing white on a beach
and sweating blood.
Maybe I'm dying,
maybe it's my time.
No, she said, we are purifying you
in our dreams.

THE SEARCH TREE

The wood is made of antler and the antler of wood.
Search tree, middle west, an arc of camera
anatomy in the shot, on the film,
the highway goes blue dim and the antelope
are horses galloping, I am changing again,
there is the expanse of loom and height,
the toss of nickel changeth into blue moth,
we are burrowing into and under the random piles
of sticks in the long pasture by the county road,
the interstitial fauna is teaching vertices,
pleasing the congregation of companymen
drinking Folger's from small cups in the
grey abyss of airport flatlands.
Bleach, beeping, jet shadow, branded visors,
instructions on how to make coffee
are whispered to you by a child (one eye closed)
in the next seat as we fly the holding pattern
above the desert jewel known as Dubai.

Poison capsules in a cookie jar
beside the register of a just-abandoned CVS
where dogs are made shaggy in the parking lot
and we all admire the concentric sky in squarefoot lake.
Have you put your mouth to the white gutter
to wait for the last thread of rain.

CROSS AND CIRCLE GAME

The infants are painted red in the St. Augustine grass.
I saw her ideal face on the dating app
and I hope she is the one that saves me.
From what will be decided in the passionate years
of our love which will include avenue and island.
Stepping over sewer grates, a New York City love,
we will take our shoes off together
in that gritty space behind the apartment door,
chainlock swinging, radiator knocking, skin dry.

The mothers wake up blistered in the coldwater flats,
but it's just a rash, we huff scratchedoff ticket foil,
we huff straight gas, now that the wick is submerged,
now that the stars are red, are black and blue,
there is celestial camouflage afoot, there are
chess magi making sudden life moves to Parcheesi,
dominoes, Mensch ärgere Dich nicht.
Do not get angry as you count the inverted cascades
of steam from large subterranean snakes
that hint at broken DNA in equinox dreams.
When we awaken life is a cross and circle game.
We send ourselves out and we try to go home,
drinking mainstream ayahuasca from bodega foam,
smoking Anglo tobacco under Roman stone,
do you think she will like my stories
do you think she will like my shoes.

SHADOW TO SHADOW

Jumping from shadow to shadow but keeping our shadow in the sun
and all those parties where the girls would kiss each other.
There were long lines of golden tallboys slanted in the coolers
of gas stations where children shrieked about their plans
and men in blue shirts counted coins in the booth of cigarette box.

Drinking sleeping and looking for sex is a complicated affair.
The textbooks were expensive, the politics obscure.
The collegiate theme park, the lolling dance of student and mime,
the pressure kegrooms of cathexis, the ability to cup a face in smoke.
It was on the wind, it was already a memory, it was a bad time
immersed in pleasure and confusion and hormonal scrawling.
It was the slow migration of leper royalty in the vast moneychange.

Love is sponsored by beer and whoever is making all this cheap wine.
On we scatter in the long ritual of migraine cultivation,
deep navigational loss in buildings, memories of MDMA holes,
breasts in their brief span without tear and sag
and decorative gourds hefted on them in fall photos.
Munching on new snacks in a Subaru or is it a Honda and waiting
for the new blade inserts, still in this skin that insists
on rotating images, now so old, now so glum, now so reflective,
when once it was just spasmatic, hungry, humid, birdfilled,
and there on the silver plate were figs, citrus maxima,
an open rubyheart, silks drifting.

THE CHROMOSPHERE

The shift in chromosphere has turned the dust to sugar.
It has turned the sand to black salt.
The right side of her face is a tall window
and in that window is a child
who leans on the sill
and she does ask the lavender fire
what they are doing to her catalogue of loves.

One drop of blood is required
to activate the reality that awaits you
after this life is complete.
Now knowing you, it will be the perfect infinite journey.
A divine architecture of high and low.
The transition to what is commonly called death
will itself be seamless.
It will be a coral blooming in the sensorium.
It will emerge from your throat.
The novel connections will at first be slow
so as to allow your archive-vehicle to acclimate
before it is all new all the time and you shudder
in the complex yet harmonious majesty
the ongoing mystery of eventblock traversal
the synchronous explosion of power zeros
the orgasmic loss of destination and terminus
when you know the harvesting of the blood drop
was itself part of that which cannot be divided
the meadow of selfbirthing ideas in the meringue void
the intercourse game of selfeating and selfvomiting
in the pale green arctic wilderness where tropical birds
caw manshapes for apes to scrawl on cave walls
—wind through the canal of hot copper and sunlight.

ANIMALS ABANDONED

Crushed not by our desire
but by the sincerity of our desire
by its naked clean weight
in the storm of another bedroom midnight.
To the vision we can only add apocrypha,
for the vision was all
for we fail what riseth
for I want you long in that bed
where I nightmared between two tall windows,
belly of raw fish.

You enter by doing.
Audacious and humble.
Splendid, stupid, long banished
to welsh fields, to sunbaked wood
turned to rock
to swedish furniture in plastic fumes.
I would bend you forward
I would pull your hair
and we would make many a child
and leave them on random corners
and we would become more desperate
and more pure
and we would become ferocious
in the secret bounty of our cruelty
and we would go deeper
and deeper
and we would be alone with each other
in hair, and sweat, and scream,
animals abandoned.

THE WORLD IS A SHARPENING WHEEL

The world is a sharpening wheel
for our skills as shoppers, knifelike,
and sharp knives are used to cut the metallic ribbons
of cutrate boxes containing celebrity cookbooks.
Which will be burnt for warmth.
Which will aid the evolution of insect pathologies.
Whose mulch will be studied by a race able to insert
themselves in any time-moment (moment finally
defined), each dot a waiting
infinity of further dots, a stylus
finding purchase in the continuum, the shelf,
an epoch of time the first and last
cubic gift for usage and rejection.
Edges rounding, edges bleeding,
borders releasing, and great walls incomplete,
to become the arsenal of invertebrates
like breathing and regenerative mushroom clouds,
golden, silent, barbarous, gelatinous in the sand,
voluminous blue and dark needed
for extension, the inflation revealed by waterproof light,
or, The Day When The Wind Stopped
The Wind That Halted The Day.

SEVERNY ISLAND

The shadows keep the blue frost of the morning
and maybe that is his soul.
Charts of the wounded and dead.
Maps of enemy territory.
Maneuvers and marching, occasional
descents into games of pride and reputation.
His walk is to the sea. His vengeance is total.
Worked full to shorten drastic figures,
the addition of number. Like our plan
with atomic efficiency. Less is more.
I am marching to Severny Island
        where my ancestors ate cold fish
        where hydrogen bombs make new heaven
to collect whatever icepack is left
to restore the wintersport economy of Andorra.

THE MASTER TIMELINE

Millennia of war and destruction are not an aberration.
Neither is the generosity in the heart circle of the inferno.
We are only beaten dogs, confused heartfast mammals
in cages and cutup bushes neath frozen wires.
On the poster in the halfabandoned mansion
is displayed the master timeline, the first spark
all the way to the firework in the left eye
of your second daughter. Along the way
are some pretty dreary genocides, fungi in smoke,
trillions of birthday parties, the birth of the word confetti.
Come with me to the red attic where I have hung the laundry.
You're just hands now but I'll make you a full person
and offer you a soft pallet and bring the one you really want.
Some guy from Virginia. Did you see that on the poster too?

LET THE BANDAGES UNROLL

The blank white letters come in blank white envelopes
addressed to no one but they find my white box.
It must be the address I'm emitting, watching videos
on joysound, how to get people a project, how to
get them antianti, in the autumn morning the house
is eradicated by machines and rebuilt instantaneously.

The people have begun to eat dogfood
and the dogs eat lobster and the cans it comes in.
Marriages are held in parking lots at night
away from the sun which reveals too much
and which telleth of the burden of our emancipation.
I am still the critic longwaiting his thesis,
greasy bag of burnt popcorn and wondering
if my eyes are greenglow in the shadow walls.
I let the bandages unroll down the street.

The transitionmongers are having their way with the loom.
Ripping thread in Victorian dustshafts and drinking mead,
drinking Gatorade and mead, making honey from ladybugs,
the ladybugs that are NSA camera drones making money,
money from adhesive thread, money from recurrent idol,
money from trees whose seeds we must gather to
make more trees to make more money of which
we must speak disdainfully as if it mattered but it does.
I would have been happy with one but two is double one.

Lazy music in the Ecuadorian place, I text her the address.
I have already eaten and I am waiting for the red dusk
to make a light of itself on the sweating yellow walls.
I am anticipating a cousin's death and its mellow sadness.
Someone in the backroom at the typewriter is just hitting
the space key and are they sending me the letters
and are they making me strike a mess from the message.

ONE MOMENT A SERIES

Through the dial television in the backroom we go
deep into the Mandelbrot set, adjusting for
tracking. The amoebic artwork on her walls
reminded me of myself, she said something I said
was cynical, she said she was speaking to
a very mature person. Two men hang out inside
the burgundy coveredbridge and in
one roadside moment that becomes a series

a purple flower is tangled in my shoelace
a cockroach oils along the pavement
and I see a small metal figurine:
cowboy on a wild stallion leaping
out of a silver moon and frozen there.
I put it in my pocket and proceed to cross
the stateline to lie with a stranger in a
small house built on a small hill.

Later, I dreamed of GPS on the fritz.
I watched as a porn star seemed to really enjoy
the uncircumcised penis going inside her.
Had I come upon a secret video. Was that
a boyfriend, a fiancé, a crush. Is there
a porn inside porn, one of love and tenderness
and truth. I put halfmoons of sausage into
the Maruchan ramen. I watched the first halfhour
of Dragged Across Concrete. I refused to believe
it was the sixth of October.

THE HANGED MAN

We never get our revenge
and if we do it is not enough.
The pain is the center point.
It is insurmountable.
It is the organizing principle.
It is the long hallway of closed doors.
The pain is the hierophant.
Without it we are useless wanderers.
We need our blood on the stone.
We need the horrific scenes
in suburban treehouse.
We need to have been tossed aside.
Nothing will undo that.
Nothing will change that.
The mechanism that allows change
has long been cut.

It gets me into the garden
but outside the fruit.
It will not let me taste
my own pallid victory.
It is the ember and the burntlands
of the valley autumn.
Fumbling in suit pockets
near the future site
of an exploding bridge.
The pain will not be taken.
The moment will not be
and cannot be
deleted, like some aberrant
letter.

You have thrown yourself
down that well
but there is no bottom.
All the bottles are one
and it's not even filled.
The pain cannot be bought
it refuses to be traded
or put on some folding table

neath the white stare
of the cracked drive-in screen.
It is not an object to be minimized.
It is the fire in the marshlands.
It is the floating rails
and the inversion of towers
in the water and the reeds
of the chemical ambrosia.
It is the flickering of bridges
and the broken antennae
in the decadent swamp
that surrounds the city of whooping cough.
Stab it but find no location
only teenage bloodsport.
Speak it but the name changes.
Kill it but it rolls the boulder of the crypt.
Throw it but it curves.
It returns.
It resides again in your belly.
It is the sphere outside time
the coordinate ever shrinking
the tea that cannot be steeped
or must be steeped forever
you must stir the risotto
for the genocidal king
in so many slippers
and yes
you must laugh with him
on the platform
of the blackhood and rope series
you must laugh and agree
that nothing has been solved
and nothing learned
and there was a pain
beyond the pain
not a buoy throwing red light
but the ocean in all its halftone
not the moon
but the fabric in which it sits
of which it is made
and now that you are the hanged man
you can see this

The Fires

and this:
the blood is a favorite of gravity
and the world is about to open.

THE BECAUSE AUTHOR

Yes, you accurate great,
imagine because up,
what plot there, total nova,
my it's Hughes from One,
what column activated,
besides Trip, reading this train.
Sure, extraordinary characters,
gunman,
  Who
forgotten—
has he read Fishpond
in already downreason direction.
There, some discover: Do Not Have I've, Does I?

Therefore, if say Program Out,
incidentally, the gray room I produced—
what made where anywhere, planet
begin, I registered around.
My most one is naked. Excuse Alexandria,
a written book that became,
but what I have is now dead thing.

Do something like amateur as voices.
Do hamburger with I.
What there was: that case.
Characters, which characters down.
Earlier world? Yes, very.
Who's been shortchanged with figure-starts.
You, even on the buzzer
in the well, in train photographs: three files,
one drawer, mean files...

I'm interested really in that time you Yes'd.
The swordsmanship. Would I character down,
the sensation a western, in characters with competence.
He, him, here, [reading]. Yes. Cattle going think:
Would he western. Dr. the do. In a sense,
would he direct brokerage.
Well by that time Jesse James was an addict.
Knew morphine... heavily addictive, genteel.

The Fires

What see in prone cry. What not notRockefeller was required,
the obtrusive, Playboy A. Ideas smoking.

Didn't you glimpse faculty copywriter accounts?
Endocreme, hormones, thoughtcornered army exterminator.
Why I menace: the automatic causes.
You're my killed and my tell.
Rewarding conditions Paris, either afternoon, war dissatisfied.
You: somewhere found York, very very odd machine,
the Rubenstein milliondollar bill.
Photograph old ashpit, society columns, names,
youtime, isolated
expense.

The better the hanging depresses the Zen,
MIT attempt occurs, manipulative much at the individual,
then God, god events for garbage, the reef of girls,
further intelligence mutations, future in from inevitably why,
between apparatus, they're control will feeling,
impossible cold, get united "right." The unions
plant the charge but it focuses you, become well.
Much what's fuck comes to know the sergeant dismantled,
and sex that human. This priori was investigated fear from
the fatherhouse, of stupid people action.
You would, because Author.

THE NEW AMERICAN TAROT

From The New American Tarot you pulled

The Bicycle Playing Cards.
The Levi's Blue Jeans.
The Joint.
The Alcoholic Father.
The Rapper.
The Sinking Mall.
The Rusted Car In The Woods.
The Chinese Food Place.
The Unanswered Prayer.

All major arcana, which is interesting,
but meaningless.
Pull again.

The Homeless Veteran.
The Ramen Package.
The Realtor.
The Motel Adulterer.
The Suicide.
The Immigrant Prodigy.
Jack Ruby.
The Slave Cemetery.
The Skyscraper.
The Surgeon.
The Pedophile Priest.
The Frozen Vomit.
The White Rapper.
The Couple That Cannot Conceive.
The Contractor.
The Scarecrow.
The Trailer Park.
The Billboard.

Major arcana. Okay. Try again.

The Manhole.
The Ghost.
The Seer.

The Flea Market.
The Thief.
The Healer.
The Hacker.
The Prostitute.
The Duelist.
The Duelists.
The Huntress.
The Eclipse.
The Hidden Well.
The Flood.
The Mountain.
The Marksman.
The Cave.
The Geometer.
The Wanderer.
The Glacier.
The Spoiled Brat.
The Red Waste.
The Traitor.
The Plague.
The Farmer's Hotel.
The Language.
The Farmer.
Alexei Lorenz.
The Subliminal Message.
The Carpenter.
The Monolith.
The Salt Flats.
The Double.
Nine.
The Trail.
The Song.
The Invisible Fox.
The Door.
The Leper.
The Arch.
The Lights In The Sky.
The Astronomer.
The Eunuch.
The Colossus.
The Strip Mall.

The Ghost Book.

We're going to need to clarify all this.
Pull again.

The Clock.
The Double.
The War.
The Bronx.
The Lonesome Howl.
The New American Tarot.
The Cicadas.
The Total Field.
The Cornucopia.
The Torch.
The New Alchemist.
The Inventor.
The Roadside Trash.
The Cartographer.
The Loom.
Seven.
Kether.
The Mandala.
The Abandoned Drive-In.
The Bones.
The Strawberry Moon.
The Twelve.
Kali.
The Patriot.
The Hollywood Blockbuster.
Seven Seven.
The Wolf Moon.
The Cold Moon.
The Dream.
The Snake.
The Coyote.
The Coup.
The Weasel.
Jupiter Opposite Jupiter.
The Egg.
The Morning Sex.
The Oracle.

The Unemployed Philosopher.
The Wall.
The Trail Of Tears.
The Lion.
The God.
The Grey Cardinal.
The Leviathan.
The Health Department.
The Circling Hawk.
The Shapeshifter.
Mickey Mantle.
The Rainbow.
The Hermaphrodite.
The Land Of Goshen.
The Cop.
The Watren Monk.
The Fortune.
The Ruins.
The Onanist.
The Vampire.
The Hardcore Band.
The Magic Bullet.
The Rusted Viaduct.
The Gideon Bible.
The Regent.
The Truck Driver.
The Dream.
The Stoner.
The Palace Holographic.
The Realm.
The Dreamer In The Dream.
The Dream Without Dreamer.
The Wildfire.
The Sanctuary.
Fort Berthold.
The Seduction.
The Sepulcher.
The Crucible.
The Danube.
The Jinx.
The 99¢ Slice.
Metacomet.

The Spy.
The Criminal.
The Pawn Shop.
The Charlatan.
The Liar.
Make Bleed The Environs.
The Prisoner.
The Stag.
Zero.
The Whirlpool.
The World Mover.
The Avalanche.
The Catastrophe.
The Aboveground Pool.
The World Dreamer.
Two Two.
The Double.

Okay. Okay.
Most of these cards I've never heard of.
But...
Pull again.
With your left hand.

I DON'T KNOW WE MADE IT RAIN

The hand of the man is shaking
and he is pointing to me
and he is saying You are not welcome here
and I simply push him off the bench.

The blue tarantula is at war with the killer fungus.
Predatory loans and Don't touch the sea turtle.
Harvesting data and eliminating the platform.
Old valentines kept in brown plastic bag.

Your good deed has become a brand strategy.
My stigmata fluid is really more of a pus.
Are those pushcarts sold at Old People Stuff.
Is there a babushka market for immigrant clichés.

We are forced to care about a world we were forced into.
Money can and often does buy happiness—
I would maybe not repeatedly demand a woman pay the bill.
I would not go into the make a human happy business.

I am growing claws to claw out my eyes.
That fostered dog will not bring you a boyfriend.
I swear that Atari started playing porn from the future.
A naked woman installed in corner for afternoon breasttouch.

Everything is natural. Nothing is outside nature.
Nature allows the machete spree. Nature is plastic.
We are all the product of egg magnetism and wombfield.
We are all the product of those Oedipal fish squiggles.

I met God and we laughed at everyone.
He is indeed fat and I pushed him in a wheelbarrow.
We designed broken babies and chuckled.
We pushed failed fathers off roofs.

We made your fiancé like better ass.
We made your mother a cellophane skin junky.
We made the iron chains that enslaved the Africans.
We made the sparkle shoelace for the shoes of tennis.

We made the team of men who fixed your gutters.
We made the individual idea of team in each brain.
We made the idea of brain in your brain.
We made the idea of an idea being in a brain.
We made the idea of change and we made the idea change
I don't know We made it rain.

THE HOLY LAND

Surrounded by wolves and specters
on the cold peak of the holy land,
alone like the moon has vanished.
The stations are corrupt, the monoliths
are returning to gravel and stone,
the ground is a patch of snow and
sallow grass. I am waiting for them
to move. I am waiting for the kill.
I have stood and shivered for
days and millennia, marking the
erotic blue eclipse and the radical
dispersal of moisture. Heaven is
tenuous, goldshot, no one answers
when I speak in my most silent tongue.
The wolves are hunger and the specters
confusion. They are the two laws,
the alternating forces a garland I am
roped in them. Shiver in the rain
and the mist of long dead fathers,
there are broken beads in the crag,
they cannot be made true and circle.
I am naked in the trial, I am centered
in the eyes, tall in the loss of energy
and the bizarre cathedral of meat,
of water and blood and of hair. It is
a mystery and it is long and cruel.
Made to eat and food, the symmetry
is fixed always, there are columns of
drool and the wolfhair is a grass in the
turning of windforms and the raising
of sentient longing, enlivened by howl
and destitute schematic, enfeebled line,
toy of milk and urge, rapacious dictum.
I was a man with tools in leather and...
now I am this bare thing, child on the peak,
a vessel of captured weather, a boned
crossing of the word, dumb arbiter
of godless momentums, they will not
give me the gift of an end just the
elongation of fear and vision, just

the subtle pulse of a mourned creation,
the clouds weighted again, the valleywater
black, birds in a forward knowledge
and I am here and I am surrounded
by wolves and specters in the holy land.

MANURE AND STRAWBERRIES

Manure and strawberries.
Who gets to tell who what to do.
Fullblooded whipped cream.
Tall blondwooden boxes dispersed in the amberfield.
Do not miss me.
I have failed many.
I am coiled in serpents.
I am still licking through tiedye ice cream.
Halfhollow, leaves in the wheelbarrow.
Breaking in the rows of shellacked coffins,
some of them redwood, some of them fiberglass.
There has been an outbreak of pillow banditry.
There has been an outbreak of infants.
Lose my number.
Tell the aliens I said Stop.
Tell the sharp dreams to descend.
Massaging out the bullet wounds.
Exercising the immoveable face
in the slew of provocateur and catmewling.
Stomping jackolanterns.
Love lives askew.
I have finally arrived.
I have put the coat to the hook.
I am not You so do not make the mistake.
I am untouchable. I am drastic.
You are here on the stonewalk to the staircase.
The cold wind is pulling apart your hair.
You want something but I am not home.
I keep telling you.
I am screaming.
The stars are coming through the morning.
There was a chariot last night,
through the trees, through the memories,
I am leaving soon, in through one ear.
Do you believe it?
Can you believe it?
Believe me.
I was never here.
You never saw me.
My birth certificate is a photocopy.
There has been a prophecy of slashes.

THE REAL RIDE

Scotchbroom and perennial shrubs
and Class B noxious weeds
against the basement window
all over the inherited lawn
allied with the buried workbench
and the cataclysmic shoulders
from the decade plus of
shrugging.

(The misspelling of dark is cark.)
I want to be the smoking cowboy
in the bower of the superstation.
He knows of the strange attractor
because he is that very thing
in the shadowhill of Stonehenge,
the embedded tablets of faded
epigrammatica,
for to rub a pocketwatch
is to expose the clockwork
and to speak in Latin
is to decloud the fatherlands
and this whole time
you have been assassinating my ka
as I have huddled beside the tree
in the parking lot of the arboretum,
sipping from one of those blue camping
cups, wellfed, wellbred,
waiting for the real ride
and clicking my new spurs,
chromium star at my heel.

THE CHILDREN OF AMBIVALENCE

Emergent in the metropolitan fallout we are bulbs in the erratic magnetic fields.
Slow glare and the rooms of parental artifact, of threads and souvenirs.
What else but the father asleep in the brown recliner, the TV blaring artificial wars.
Mothers and their binders of recipes, mothers and their lives of quietus.
They made children to have friends forever but the enemies are close to behold,
the young handed to strangers to recite engravings and to make a drug of dealers.
Grown here like another crop and put into the leviathan hypnosis,
the tone and the humor and the pride and the pattern and the code and the history.
Urged to care and to feel for the dead and the unseen living, for the long chain
of ancestors who toiled, of slaves who boiled, we only inherit the stupor,
we are only real in debt, if ye do not obey the law the law will snuff ye.
There is a steady indifference that the market and military aim to eradicate.
Passion is not our home, we have a sense of its body count,
we have a sense of the blood acreage of Jerusalem as we spoon heroin
and trade diabetes paraphernalia, we were only ever cannibals in denim and leather.
Brought to the longstanding death camp and outraged when we die.
Pitched into the rape world and baffled when we are invaded and seized.
Raised in the eternal war to weep and marvel at the need for supersonic jets.
This is the location of the atrocity. The atrocity is nowhere else.
Each of us reprimanded for failing a league of designs, the family crest,
the stitch of flags, the mutants of custom. We have not been good friends,
we have been miserable lovers, we have been flawed thinkers,
we have been pretty pathetic citizens, we have been addicts and buyers,
we have been abused and neglected and we have been completely forgotten,
we have been caressed and kissed and our pleasures have been interrupted
and we want them back and we are prepared to sleep. It is a perfect world,
ignorance is the dominant trait, it is a belowtree somewhere in the grey jelly.
Existence is slavery. It is a fractal field of slavery. We do the work of a barren force.
We do the work of a barren force and we are dying from overwork,
but the work did provide fellatio and chocolate so resume the jog fair child.
We do sometimes choose what will carry us out of this orbital mess,
tending to the desires that we did not choose, in the realm of perceived choice
born of the supreme lack of choice. We are ghosts that never lived, it is that benign,
it is that juvenile cafeteria where the computer teacher rubs your shoulders.
We are the offspring of a shrug and an accidental or purposeful spurt
but you still take everything so personally, it's still so serious and hot.
We are the regretted. We are the superfluous makers. We are the caregivers
and we are the ragged ambivalent. We were simply not aborted.
We're miracles too as long as we behave and do make love less conditional.
The rings of Saturn are around your head, I can see your bones,

God the abusive boyfriend you keep sucking off after every profound smack.
God the witch mother slowly raising the temperature of your bath in the cauldron.
Be sure to vote fair child. Be sure to pig. Be sure to recycle. Be sure to self.

THE ROAD AGENTS

Don't you miss the kids on milk cartons?
In the stillness of our disasters the echoes sound
like an old prude. No electricity. What exists now?
I would love to come back as the urn for your ashes.

Moths... Other than flames where do they go?
Cupboards, Dakota blackwater.
The collapse of resonance, the gematria
of your palm. I'm not sick, you're sick,
we're both sick. We have ingested the last
stick of TNT, supernumerary, the soft click
the katana makes in its scabbard of high polish.

That naked man is throwing flowers in the widowed field.
That man has buried himself in the basement of false trees.
People walk right up to me and scream.
We flap packets to collect the contents so we can tear
where it says to tear, there are dotted lines,
there is perforation, we follow the arrows,
we do yield and we do slide, we desire a mistress when we
come upon the sign for detour, there is a countdown,
and when the double bars of yellow on separate hills align,
the road agents of the highway and the ronin of the plains,
the geishas of the motel and the whores of the rain,
all become white-aproned gardeners to rejuvenate and tend
the ruined bonsai garden of youth, yours.

IN LIEU OF FLOWERS

At the behest of magic foxglove
I am trying to be a bed-on-fire
optimist, instead to be
a man on perpetual fire
at The Henry Ford,
near Jesse James on ice,
between JFK's black deathlimo
and Honest Abe's
eerie bloodthrone
convulsed by
operatic singing.

In lieu of flowers
I am at the whim of the six of cups
and the CD of Red Medicine.
To have the audacity of the offspring
of cardinal and flamingo
but to free myself from
the circle of animals
after ingesting a boatlike leaf
from the surface of the river Lethe,
or to find the merkhaba
in the depths of the lint trap,
to reach out in hypnagogic spasm
to read the crop circles
like so much fallen braille
and to open the user manual
in the glovebox of the ethereal body.
In my typical backpack
the founder's bones,
on my head
the disintegrating kaftan
as I walk through
the hole in the ice.

A heightening of compliments
is an eschatological sign.
A deepening of reliance
a worm in the bottle of wine.
He closed his eyes before I shot him.

The Fires

He made good use of his worry beads.
We are riven, he said,
at the séance on the dock,
where the reflected edge of the treeline
is a broken north.

THE OVERLAP OF THE VEN

You are the overlap of the ven,
the pole not the flags,
which is why the adepts underscore
the importance of the erect spine.

A guy hatched in the eighties.
The answer to a mother's prayer.
A baby then. A man now.
Euro if you can see.
I am the one who sleeps.
I am the axis and submission of I.
Moneyed guzzler. Clothed eater.
Precarious sexual partner as if
we are about to make a deal.
Let's make a deal:
I am not the constant scope of black flies.

How often is this heaven-earth bridge I?
It is eu. It is yo. It is a brother of 1,
an accurate reflection of the botched doppelgänger.
But I is right because I know it as the bare axismundi.
I know it as the Greek column that floats
down the hallway of doors aligned.
The matchstick representation of the relieved integer.
The upraised arm in fresh escape from the negatives
and the weighted absence of the curve mystery.
The last ditch of the claw before cliffdeath.
It is the fang. It is the slim tornado
that collects the homes and vehicles and livestock.
It is the dark weatherform that is here
before it deforms, before it is again collapsed
to a line and feared. It is the goat pupil now yang.
It is the profile of the gear of dreams.

THE GALLERIA (DA LAT)

Or the woman in black at the Subaru dealership.
They are raising bread in the last golden bakery of the river city.
Dawn, zigzags of rust, thinking of Da Lat
and the blue morning street like a new form of ice.
She is another woman waiting for love
in the gentle voice of her mother and the diningroom
table arrangement ruled by division, by the
irrefutable need to keep track of everything.
Shredders are on sale and digital chemicals
that dissolve your identity so you can
eat bowls of hot pho where the couples ride plastic
swans in the slow circle collection of
water bodies.

The pandemic galleria still carries many ballcaps.
JCPenney is where your mother has chosen to haunt.
Another protest is right on schedule.
The white jeans are in my size and I have bought them
through the clerk who says we are now in a red state.
It's been like this, she says, meaning slow.
She is not implying anything other than the metronome
that clicks mute but distinct somewhere in Filene's Basement.
Black Xs on the menu for the salon the salon close to
the arcade the arcade close to the corner optician.
Have they installed a Vietnamese place in the food court?
Are we there yet? Is there anyone I can ask?

And if I asked her out would we pass the redemption center?
There are Spirit Deals. There is an Airbnb for my friend's
birthday party and comingout ceremony as an intuitive healer.
What am I going to do with two sweatshirts?
What am I going to do with this shaking fist and you?
Are we a generation that speaks in rhetorical questions
and must continually make peace with our fathers?
Do we say O before we list examples?
Do we say O before we lift our voices to monologue?
Do we call our mothers bimbos, offhand?
After the rains it is best to look for arrowheads.
Before the rains it is best to blow the gutters.
I've been in love with a few cutters,

chased them and bored them and followed them
and discovered why they may have done the minute slashing.
Are we a generation that cannot be trusted with knives
with nice knives with nice things?
For once just answer me.

THE SURFACE OF JUPITER

There has been the internal error.
There is a steel ghost in the atmospherics.
The spykites are increasing their skypresence.
You are telling me that there is a passion lacking, a heat.
I agree and it's back to the crypt of clock and boffo.
A brain came to shore in a helmet of tinfoil.

Lightdrunk suzerains and the manifestation of the love sphere.
Azteca chairs a very dark and polished brown.
Lay the white napkin on your thigh and thank the trees.
I jab a needle into the air to summon the base materia
which is the milky surface of Jupiter where our dreams
are wave and protoplanet, are bubble, where they come from,
they are information apertures with cool minds and the necessary
images that architect the contents of sectioned time now melting.
Check your pocket for the note I beamed to you:
I am dead serious.

I am now winking to you as the needle becomes full.
I am jabbing the needle into the wood that is a tablet
and the grain is a roiling picture language
and the grain is now everywhere
and you smile and the white substance is freed from your teeth.
The needle blurs over its bounds and is now gone,
is here but diffused into the dream injection,
the empty of manic color and gradation
and there, now, what about that,
what about that that I can do.
The server comes and these drinks are on the house.
I have changed everything by making it slightly better.

THE CONSPIRACIES

The cellphone companies are in cahoots with the hand doctors.
The stinkbugs are robotic spy units and the ladybugs use active
sonar to make accurate models of reality scene and suspect room.
You are in love with a German man who is obsessed with marathons.
I was locked into the service industry by an exacting network of bad actors.
Google has raided my emails-to-self and has perverted my global designs.
I am an alien scientist in human form but the amnesia program is whacked.
Buddha is an interdimensional führer trying to cripple us through stasis.
Members of Beatles were/are primitive AI units bloomed in nonsequential time.
Complaint is a definite frequency and the universe relies on it for continual growth.
Flowers are bad for the human retina and lead to erectile dysphoria and dry pussy.
Humans only need water but are sick on this point, hence, beverage managers.
Maggot the father of the fly and maggots are truelords in this soil regime.
Death is the perfect synthesis of your fantasies and boy won't your face be red.
Existence makes itself as it goes along to accommodate its own investigations
(see: proton collider, the amoeba, gut flora, neutrinos, many worlds, cell wall).
Existence makes intuition so it can shrug at its own counterintuitive truths.

THE PHONE BOOTH OF EVIDENCE

In the phone booth of evidence the tacks
are bridged by string, there are photographs
of suspects and bystanders innocent
who I have made guilty through trees of personage,
my scribbling, quotes to divide the numbers
of height, there are photocopies, there is
doppelgänger innuendo, prophet book of statistic,
and when I leave the accumulation of pulp and reference
the air is so clean my lungs recoil, they kick.

Can't help looking back, can't help
inviting the mood, in five years it will be
a complete and definite failure
and I may lose an inch or two of my legs.
Can't look up to those windows
where I used to massage your legs on my lap
before we gave each other the look
and went into the slanted bedroom.
I used to hide out in libraries
I used to perfect my cling wrap
around the small salads that became vertical discs
arranged in the fridge of the vegetarian restaurant
where lesser celebrities would hide out
where we would cut big slices of cake
and eat behind the sweating taps
in our grungy corner of paradise
in the one-street progressive enclave
the trees tall and leaning over the strip
and we would take Daniel bowling
before returning him to the home
of men who have no home
but at least have this, the house behind the restaurant.
The young servers and washers and cooks
dream of the icons they will become to shatter
other icons as they dip bread into seasonal soup.

Ghosts wandering in aboriginal dreamtime,
matter is never created therefore it can never
be destroyed (but it is). Two brothers
or clone lovers on a tandem bike,

one in red, one in blue, the jokes are clacks
in the long stream of sadness and carousel.
We drive and judge the houses, she calls
the one place burntcampwoodblack sexy.
We are apartment people, I say, we are
people who eat pastries and do odd jobs
for acquaintance and cousin. We are
mild centers of self. We don't know anything
and we live for all kinds of dead, waiting to collapse
back into the service industry, twisting mopheads
and reading Carver and arguing
with shift managers in their halos of cologne.
Is there still a service industry, what givens
are our visions of the future based on
what do they sit on
the twin towers burned on top of
the black metal tower in the highschool
classroom, the exalted television,
the report in glowbands on the execution
of the shadow of the implications of ideas,
the doubling and tripling of the age of anxiety,
the home never home, the ways and waves,
of course we fed the alcohol industry
of course we made millionaires of the
heirs of Fender and Gibson and Peavey
and we tussled in the shade of the trees of the bad guys
the white teeth of the millennium-edge politician
we came here to come here we imagine
our lives as abortion and stillborn
but we are mostly sure to wrap it up
and we are mostly sure of what we are doing
and we are mostly sure of what it means to do.

The Fires

NATIONAL WHOLESALE LIQUIDATORS

It is the candy fennel in the vacuous lobby
of the Indian restaurant in the multifloored stripmall
diagonal to the yellow National Wholesale
Liquidators, the red oil rising in the food you add
to rice. Do not tempt me.

There are always traffic circles and there are dead pigs
in fuming rivers beneath moribund skies
that occasionally let slip a white Himalaya peak,
monkeys orange in a sleep pyramid, sunning
in the brief light.

Now this windowscreen
where we can watch the rain on the vertical walls of leaf
like bloated gingko that have exploded their elegance,
sad treasuries, sad deliverance, mechanical hubris,
no bills in the open guitarcase of Budapest,
we are paying the cost of the proliferation of stuff.
Black trunks, green vine-rope on black fence.
The spam callers must have a number to dial.

It was the week of losing the idea of friendship.
We used to have so much to say, or at least the need to speak.
Dimwitted bassists and manic barbacks permanently lost
in service ghettos, in MP3s mistitled.
Feed the healing rock moonlight and so I put it
on the white windowsill.
Not everything can be a Japanese paperhouse.

BY THE LIGHT OF THE BLOOD MOON

And if the world does not reward your efforts
you will dust it for fingerprints
by the light of the blood moon.

And if you are a fugitive from love
you will drink tarcoffee in private concerts of regret
as the morning sun burns the night mist.

And if the bodies are stacked on your rented lawn
and they are kept in black bags without identification
you will hope there is a service to remove them.

And if you will go on solitary and envious
through the chamber-rotation of sound and scream
you will keep winks from God in a small notebook.

And if you will not be born with confidence and cool
you will have to make it from Hollywood props
by the light of temperate suns.

And if you will not stand you can sit upright
in the eateries and delicatessens of the valley
and you can pretend you always wanted this, like this.

And if you will be vague the confusion will be earned
but if you are clear the vision will be myopic
by the ghost light of the bay and its secret coyote.

And if you will not give her your hours and dreams
she will find a man with a good job and tattooed skin
and they will laze in tropical bedroom to the perpetual hush of wave.

And if you will not even give the world a plan to ruin
you will begin the circuit of collection and cough
by the good and true light of the blood moon.

THE UNKNOWN SESSIONMAN

Unknown sessionman
picking wild oregano and sea oats
and goldenrod and other growth
he does not know
near the yellowy sheep
nosing their way across the field
where certain haybales are covered
in white plastic.
A bulb will burst in his mind
as he awakens on the deflating air mattress
and it will have nothing to do
with the window that could have been opened.

Lightning behind
the time and temperature building
and there is the periodic scream
of three in the afternoon
and the periodic scream
of three in the morning.
The heroes we thought we would be
vanish within us
as we realize we have consented
to the realities of the maniac
and the fearful soul
and the imprisoned soul
here on the vast anonymous plain.

Day O. Star O.
Dreams anticipating conversation subjects
as Belafonte turns on the table
and the isolated thunderstorm
enshrouds the plateau
as the gigantic dog
comes into the room
as if called
and stands to match
the saltandpepper hair
of the unknown sessionman.

THE HANDHELD RADIO

Still that mute kid
roaming the woods and the hills
circling the culdesacs and tracing the streets
holding that batteryoperated handheld radio.
Still turning pints of golden beer
in jukebox bars where the darts are thrown
and where those wooden bowls are found
to hold the snacks you have forgotten.
You turn to see the queen of the college cafeteria
staring at you.

It is okay if you want to punish me.
We are never going to Hawaii.
I will not manifest a powerful appreciation
for telescope and crypto.
No, just this,
the era of dial and switch and high button
the era of other touch and how fast dimensions are lost.
Change is not always progress.
I would have to agree still walking
beneath the crescent phase
or the constellations I do not want to know.
There are walkers. There are sailors.
There are those who waited for the song to come on
and listened for messages in AM static.
There are those who cover their windows in foil.

THE CHILDREN OF JOB

The children of Job
but we never had the flocks to lose.
Now we wander through
the orchard of paperbark cherry.
It is still free to see.
It is not free to touch.

There is joy in the juggling.
Thoughts must be kept and followed.
He complaineth and he reacheth
a high plane, a diamond poetic.
You can see him merging
with the ground of blasted rock
and fallen antler and broken seed.

Our comforters are indeed failures.
Stirring dirty chai and watching us,
thinking the future can still be plussed
by the genius of entrepreneurs.
To you the future looks like...
a black hole.
No. It is not that.
It is completely neutral.
She seemed to like that even less.
At least a hole is a thing
and the Arabic city
is a radiant profile of the script.

THE SOLDIERS

When the soldiers came they humiliated the fathers.
In their perfect uniforms they tore the ground
and they watered the ground and they enabled mud
and they put the fathers into the mud and naked the fathers crawled.

The soldiers drove in ravenblack Ford Mustang Fastbacks.
They knifed sausages and they grilled in our parks.
Their kindness to women was verbose, exorbitant,
but it had a precision that made us wonder.
All while the fathers crawled and froze.
All while they did terrible things in the black snow.
All while they pulled the frosted dead on long toboggans.

The local kings dethroned our acquiescence was ensured.
They took the money out of the banks and then they took the banks.
The fathers that survived the grotesquerie were simply shot.
The conditions for dreaming began to deteriorate
and we realized they were the luxury of a nowgone era,
the era itself was a dream and now we were awake.
By giving us a new set of problems, the soldiers solved our old
problems, and their greater army was victorious,
and their flag was lifted, and we were the spoils.

I did not think intestines would look like that, vaguely floral.
The soldiers were installed in our homes.
The uniforms were folded and put into closets and drawers.
There were rumors of actual love, of better domesticity.
I admit, after the initial carnage, life was smooth,
they were masters of the transition, they were very careful.
Of course I am still trying to raise the dead
with an occult backgammon box that can float on the creek.
Yes, we all remember, we know it unjust,
but the soldiers know there is no justice,
only the will to cause trouble, the will to make a dream real.

THE PSYCHO HISTORIAN

Skull on the desk.
Tick on the lip.
The yellow leaves are falling.

I stumbled upon the pope.
I closed the red zipper.
The first ever hurricane duo.

I cannot stand it when you talk bad about yourself.
We doused our lives in nutritional yeast.
We watched Buffy in the attic apartment.
Planned Parenthood was across the street.

Friends wanted you.
Men screamed at you.
Is your beauty a curse to you?

BACK FROM THE DEAD!

Put back into the dust
to watch explosion footage
to dream of execution
by Appalachian creek.

Proof of income.
Pre-order blues.
The driveway will be sealed
so park on the street
for 24 hours.

Back from the dead!
the dentist says
apropos of nothing
and he charges me
three hundred fiftyfive dollars.

When the computer multiplies files.
When the rent is negotiated.
When the expresident speaks.
When people look stunned
and afraid
and we begin
the comparison
of misery.

BLADES OF THE FEAR DISTANCE

We know now that we are blades of the fear distance.
Out in the sun the stalker we cut our wax statues with tin tools.
We are less than forgotten because we were never seen.
Our sex dreams have become blood dreams, antimedia dreams,
we would like to stuff money into the mouths of our enemies
and light ourselves on fire in the backyard of the landlord.
We are wombmad and capricious and our violence is our only security.
Our bones are vibratory. Our hope is a thin banner of the past.
We are the regenerative complex.

We roll balls of skin and we do not accept your amazing predictions.
We are haunted and endowed and we know the secret words.
We will roam these canyons and set them ablaze
and have you seen the fractal madness of rivers of fire.
We know the topography and law of the dream in the dream.
We will use Lyme disease to cripple your children.
We pilot the alleys and the decrepit taverns.
We have turned geometry on itself to curve limits and distort heritage.
You have put us here, you have set us here, our garments are of dust,
you have laid a noose round our feet.

We froth, we belly, we scribble messages from lost stars.
We know that to stop is to gain fat and inferior death.
We are hopelessly neutral we are starving romantics we are chaotic loners.
We are deep losers in the ching and bam of arcade drugs.
We know the false static of reality and we know the poison of eye.
We have guzzled gin at your weddings and coughed ash at your ceremonies.
You cannot hide even in time, we have infected the eons.
True viral and carnivorous spore, each one of us a lion steelblue,
death is a permanent vacation from this knit misery.

God has swallowed one too many grapes whole
and now it is time to choke on the seeds.
We will not pool and swamp we will light and wind.
There are two forces within the whole and you know what we are.
Devastation, the tyrannical comedy of change, the destructive volt,
our grievances will not be unheard, we are not wilted.
Smoke enclosing the gallows we are vagina dentata and the crimson scythe.
We blind you with our wailing and the diamondbeams of our complaints.
We are powerfully useless, a heart of stasis.

Have you heard a scream so pure it turns to shrapnel.
We are alone in the glow and putrefaction.
We do lurk in your email and we appear as lepers in your virgin sheets.
You have summoned us. We have called ourselves up.
It is the appearance of the vacuum, the star in the microwave.
We were meditated into chimeric beasts by deathmonks sheathed in black silk.
We are gleeful and ecstatic in the palatial waste.
We move closer and closer to the macro abyss and to the behemoth jaw.
Teeth serrated, our fidelities and connections are strong,
our chemicals and serums are strange, mystifying, pharmacological quanta.
We will feed the jaguars coffee and meth at the door of the nursery.
We will quake you with drone and bell and strong chime,
skulls floating on the reservoir meniscus, dead sparrows in your gutters.
We have constructed you out of closet matter only to skin you
and decorate the trees whose names we will banish in the feed.

The Fires

THE MERMAID

I can never tell anyone
how I worshipped your nipple and breast
with the portal of my mouth
and touched your lips
with slow dedication
and heard you moan Oh my god.
I make you again every day.
To delight and expire.
I keep your tone and I resurrect your color.
You told me crazy things in the plaza.
You want to be a mermaid.
You told me your real name.
You grew bashful and said
I'm sure you felt how I excited I was.
I massaged you to sleep,
you called it your Figaro moment,
we never met again.

LET THE TURTLES EAT THE FLESH

Pencil shavings in the bowl of cereal.
We are only explaining left
to someone who cannot
understand left and right.
Even the L his fingers make
will not do.
So we toss the ramhead into the pond
and let the turtles eat the flesh.
We drink wine. We clean pools.
We march rocky hills
and read the staid reportage
of dead generals.
We are learning to be humble.
God likes a humble worker
and the social worker learns
that the migrant workers suffer
most during wreath season.
We are watching a young mother
pretend to be a train
between the red rails.

BE LUCKY

Be lucky.

The advice beneath the advice.
The real secret. The only secret.
The void egg, the hidden erection,
the clandestine well of the sages,
hustlers, gurus, conquerors, the prophets.
The empty truth we will build a library
to encircle, so we do not have to say it.

If you are failing, I would suggest
being born as someone who does not fail.
Or being born as someone
who has the ability to stop failing.
But you were born you
and the rest is cascade mechanics.
Not your fault.

Just stop. Call it a strategic retreat.
Someone has to not do it, in fact
most have to not do it
so the rest have something to do.
It is only turning the compost
in New Orleans
after the big hurricane.
A man named Catfish
will bark at you
and demand your work
at 5 a.m. sharp
but he will not be there
and you will clear the rotting wood
from a man's house
and he will have nothing to offer
except tears and beverages
as you remove his life
and pile it in the street.

WILDFIRES IN THE CALIFORNIA BED

Amnesic waters.
Hard blue streets in the dawn
where men fold themselves in arched doorways.
Playing with her bellybutton ring
on a high mountain
and hearing the train
far below
across from the small island
where the castle of rust
is circled by a white boat.

When I let go the buildings collapse.
Somewhere Adriatic.
The fireworks factory is on fire.
Tapping the golden water
to create ring upon ring
from the comfort of the
wooden throne halfsubmerged.
A pleasurable yawn that extends the ages.

Wildfires in the California bed.
You treated your dog like a husband.
Is there anything worse than conversation?
The dance of constant interruption.
Donutshaped C code.
People do not want to listen
and they barely want to say.
We all echo the first bore.
Limp negotiations for what?
We still refuse to sleep.

You let me into your wide home
and I slept on the air mattress
in the other room, Salinas near.
We drove in the green fields
and I met your friends
and you seemed to circle one another:
people getting used to people.
I stood against the tall beach rock
and you grinded against me

in the clear wind of Big Sur
and we met in Patagonia.
We were married for a few days
and clamored for divorce
in the restaurant and plateau of California
but today I miss you.
We both had eruptions of kindness.

THE OAXACA THIEVES

The Oaxaca thieves stole my paper fortune.
I cherished it for years, kept it in other objects,
and it came from the Buddhist temple
at the foot of the city bridge.

The ram scrotum and the nest of the paper wasp,
seeing an arc of light above the night trees,
crashing UFO, paralyzed satellite, cold beer,
close comet and spark, do you ever sense your mother around?
The ghost blew in my ear, the ghost sat next to me,
the ghost knocked three times,
the movie theaters are open but not the beaches.

On San Pedro I experienced a deep gratitude,
finally, after years of cursing, I asked my
usual questions and was stopped by a presence
who said (through feeling) all I had to do
was say Thank you. So: thank you.
I'm not sure for what, but thank you.
Being useful by trying to prove
how our efforts are useless, screamed at
by an angry driver, a bystander
offered his condolences: What a bitch.

THE EXOPLANET

The pain comes from an exoplanet.
From half a planet cut by the edge
of the known and the unknown.
It is half steeped in universe
and half steeped in the substance
beyond our imagination and
conception and
beyond the ability of matter.

It is a slow pulse.
It is a slow and powerful pulse.
It awakens me to profound disgust.
It makes me know I am a visitor on this
other planet, tragic sphere, mess of interests.
The pain is a reminder and a teacher
in void league and rampant grasping,
the cunning necessities,
the broad lapping of a wolf nature,
infants crushed and sallow
and put under markers of the ground.
Why here in this weak vessel, carrier
of bruised wind and blooming distortion,
the signal proves I am a wanderer
and an arson of realities, my gospel
harsh on the ears of the slaves of this world
and its particular measures, the stack
of hollow mysteries.

Maybe I am employed by a stellar enemy.
Maybe I am the work of an edge being.
Does it tell me to detonate through boredom.
A realm of food and hunger and feeble pleasure,
small gasp and jerk, cost in cells,
shrill concepts of award and equanimity
when not one knows a thing.
Just eating and turning, or the dim brother
of a complete rainbow, the chemicals are strong here
and the message of the pain is sometimes lost.
I too grow confused and enamored.
I feast and become passionate, tossing objects.

I find myself speaking their words.
I find myself stunned with pictures
of impossible vista and delicious cure,
distracted from the cycles of deprivation,
the paltry seductions that however prove to be
unavoidable, magnetic, this stratum of lures,
gauntlet of bacteria and curses ultraviolet.
The breaking of bone and the scattering of pillar.

DELOREAN COLOR

Driving through a Tokyo videogame at night
and listening to the sound of wind
caught in a stone pavilion.
Jeweled chains make distance a truth
and the distant lights are loosening in the neon heat.
These austere cigarettes were forged in a desert
but the tobacco is fragrant and maraschino
and she will leave you tomorrow in a jet
the color of a DeLorean.

The pilots are drunk and they wander
from booth to booth in search of
noodles and women
and I have counted four rolling cups.
When we sat next to the men
they would not stop looking at you,
the doctor who wants a change in life.
There was a slave cemetery out there
where the blue makes a cloud and apple trees,
and you can imagine the headstones
trying to straighten, to brighten,
if they are even there
past thin meridians of barbed wire.
Your eyes blink so slow and we are cramped in here
trying to eat our food so neat
your eyes big and white
in your brown freckled skin
and the men will not stop looking at you.

THE WHEEL OF POLTERGEISTS

We will be humbled in the wheel of poltergeists
and we will be made poltergeist in our own lives.
We will make interests to work against
to talk of weather with the hardware clerk
working our credit cards near the tower of key implement.

I needed to not hear my voice for a few days
and I lost a beautiful woman in the recess.
Ah, well, the breath is still on our shoulders
and we are chased through the streets
with old furniture on the curb.
POWMIA flag and the stars and stripes
intertwined and sagging like banana fruit.
The curtains in the windows are magnified doilies
and the other window is packed with blue attendant shirts.
There is a Japanese art, of course,
for enlivening the grain by burning the wood.

It is the economy of having to know a guy
but we have to admit, watching the business fail,
that existence has always been quite honest with us,
but what does it mean to have an intense hypnic dream
of a circuit board, the chips painted clowncolor—
technology is a sad punchinello.
Or did it really mean the city heart of the electric fan
would indeed fail, as it did, hours later in the night.
Waking up hot, the air still.

GREENVILLE

You are where the memories meet
and where the crickets are heard.
Have you dreamed of this man?
You are arrested for becoming
this man.
All those staples in the telephone pole
like the story of metallic society
rising from the villages of oak
like the story of the plague of rust
which is now upon us.
I remember the ghost and cotton streets of Greenville.
I remember the young royalty of the porches
and I remember how the matches
would make a night of chins
and we can still hear Job
and he does hold Hamlet
in the rented rooms of southern towns
lit by penny candles,
please do not play my new records
before I have listened to them.
We are finally without blame
licking the ceilings of our mouths
trying to get the fan to roll again
and there was always change
beneath the cushions,
certain people went on to big bands,
that guy on that diet of raw meat,
spooning it in the kitchen,
and she ended up making out with
the guy with the pirate patch.
We needed a spray to get the engine started
and when we were restless
from chess and cafe
we climbed a mountain in Boulder
and we drank of the light
after the rise and I remember it,
this is where the memories are
and where they pass,
you are where you pass through
and you ready the correct change

and you make a ball of it
for the metal net fastened
to the green tollbooth.

THE NEPALI MATCHBOX

I would like to arrive with days to spare
in Cinque Terre and where else.
It is all a heavy Italian train.
It is a rattling trainbox going uphill
on the cobblestone of Lisbon
where I ate octopus at the high counter.
It is a Nepali matchbox given to Anthony
and I hope he still has it in Chicago.
It is a flipbook of vibrant LSD tabs
each centered on a black page
in a dreamed of drug shop
in a future Santa Fe of abundant shade
where cafe trains do roll lit within
by enhanced mellow light from the twenties.
It is when I would read the JCPenney catalogue
simply to know the names.
It is when I would read the Nissan manual
to know the parts and the way of diagram.
It is the coffeebreath lawyer
who taught me about architecture
and I drew one line for the bulletproof glass.

AMERICAN EPHEMERA

The JFK assassination is when physical beauty lost
to faceless intelligence.

Avoiding sugar will take care of most of your problems
except now having nothing to live toward.

The German word for always disappointed by fireworks
but going to them anyway.

A reflection with noticeable lag is the surface deciding.
The imprecise echo that tells you what to say next.

The factory factory, darkbrown skin
against mintgreen shorts.

The heiress to a walnut fortune never did ask me
to run a restaurant in Mallorca.

What is it to be raised by babysitters?
What is it to be raised by women?
What is it to have feared men
while wanting something obscure from them?

A man sitting on a long saw
as it makes a panel from a huge sycamore.

Washing your face in the bowl of coins your hands make.
And the rivers are heavy and slow under the bridges.

Walking into an empty basketball court,
securing a fruit pie in the pocket of a JanSport.

California is thinking of California
and the open breeze of a ranch house, a saucer of almonds.

Dogs in gentle slumber under the eaves of the station
and men ponder the stacked clouds of the plains.

We drive slow like killers and cross the rails
of outer Philadelphia, on our way to sandwiches.

The Fires

Flash paper in the Indian paintbrush,
bracts of blood below the exotic katsura.

The beautiful Venezuelan woman running over circular haybales,
cunnilingus and the smell of chicken Top Ramen.

The twin houses sitting in garbage,
the construction site called a concentration camp.

Big white mushrooms so sudden
and his father helped him bring up the guns from Florida.

Science is real magic and we all come to hate real magic
because we still have to floss and we still cannot sleep.

Gritty piano samples in hiphop songs
and daydreaming of murder, sex by cobalt river.

Aborted teeth like pieces of burnt coral,
approaching the echofield of the lower level
of the George Washington Bridge.

Has the success been worth your failure?
Birds scratching while you read a colon.

There is no time left and I wonder what happened
to that Timex watch I bought at Walmart.
Is it frozen at the exact moment God forgot us,
hundredths of a second floating above the mud of pearl.

EULOGY FOR THE FATHER

This is the place where fathers die.
In this place that allows place
and in this place that promises only
sickness and death
another father has died.

He was a son begotten by another father.
He was the made and he became the maker.
He was loved and he was hated
and he slept in rooms that are no longer here
and he is no longer here
except as memory and image
and it may be that those too will perish
to give him another death.

He came here innocent
and he did leave here with crimes
some recorded in law
and some beyond the word.
He was indeed judged
and he judged in kind.
He was indeed flawed
but only if we measure him against
a better man, and that man against
a perfect man
whom we each create
and who does change
in the aspects of our sorrow and joy.

His body is now long and asleep in the earth.
Some are saddened and some relieved
and some are no different.
Some envy his new state and some are reminded
of their ongoing mortality
in this place that allows place
and allows the cherishment or hatred
of itself.
There is nowhere else for fathers to die.

He did eat food and he did make love

The Fires

and the sun did shine on him
on the land contained between
invisible borders, changing borders,
and he is buried with his secrets
some of which we may come to know.
I understand he liked some parts of this place
and disliked others
but he was a child
and he did come from a mother
and it is the children of this place
who did raise him
and he raised them in kind.
He did sweat. He did dream.
He was born on a farm and he died in a city
and if he comes to you now it will be as a ghost.

THE SECOND

THE HOMELESS MEN

The second to last time I fell in love
I conserved my semen and my energy
and when I came on the blue breasts
that had saved my life
she purred and called it a lake.

We are not free.
But we are free to speak platitudes.
There are terminal conjunctions
outside of our overheating computers
and soon we will bathe our computers
in nutritious goo.
Advertencia my dear,
things are more boring
than they appear.

Rattling around in the great earthskull
we are concrete ghosts, it merely takes
a twisting of definition.
And we are free to do that too.
And we are free to say Boo
to an unsuspecting language
grown about gates that creak
and cabbage that blooms. Hopscotch gauntlet
to the final abandoned house.
Yes, homeless men were here
and they have pissed on the flaming
letters of your name, slightly rearranged.

I wrote DEATH near the plants
and the plants began to die.
I wrote DEATH near the children
and the children began to fly.

PREWAR

We live up in the screened windows in these towns by summer rail.
We nap on made beds as the breeze comes through.
We empty ourselves in these small tiled bathrooms.
We make flowers stand in garagesale vessel.
We stand before landscape paintings we have just noticed.
We use electric percolators.

We are always prewar.
We are always worried about parking.
There is always a lonely man on his lawn with a rheumy dog.
After the camps the gums of the survivors were in better health.
Polite English scientists tell us we're fucked through numbers.
A mother dries her hands with a handtowel
and she has perfected her pignoli recipe
and she has the feeling she is underappreciated.
The train comes through Peekskill.
The kids on the bench are yelling about dicks.

I did not notice the felled trees in the backyard.
Traffic blew through the caution tape.
A woman that lives in a basement wants to fuck.
You are back from The Netherlands
and the Dutch are the most boring people alive.
Blend the watermelon with the 100 Conejos mezcal.
See the first flying cockroach you have seen here.
You hope it is the only,
uploading another document to New York State Health
and there is a white spot on your gums.

The windshield wipers do need to be replaced.
The education system does need to be fixed.
Someone would love to repair that beach house
as we celebrate mashed coconut
and wait for the light to change.
Look how beautiful the heartwood of the walnut.
Look how the archaic wire sags
and look how the teenager huffs that rag.
He wants to move to Toms River
and can you believe these Jersey drivers
and that greenlight is only thirteen seconds.

You must finish that book before Sunday.
The wifi is still out.
The kimchi did not go bad.
The sky looks different.
There is a Rosicrucian science of initiation.
Lucifer is the lightbringer.
She likes when things are named after planets.
There is a street for Sherman.
There is a street for Grant.
You are guided by Uranus.
Two million people dead is not our problem,
eight billion people alive is our problem.
Enjoy it while it lasts,
the power of now,
this world belongs to the insects.

LONG BRANCH

Wave hiss.
The sand is brown sugar.
She is in her red one-piece.
The white cloud is the white belly
of the chipmunk I crushed
yesterday on the trail.
I also ran over a snake.
We joked it would merely inflate itself
back to life.

Are these our last days?
You lay pebbles on my arms and legs
so I can absorb the rock power.
When a leaf or stone is isolated
its unique majesty does shine.
Context. Background. Environs.
These do change the object.
Your face is behind your long hair.
We discuss dead parents
and Nora's father died this morning
somewhere in Africa.
Diabetes.

The water is pulling us to the left
unless we turn and we go right.
It is pulling us north.
It is pushing us up the coast.
Lifeguards are always twirling whistles.
We found the sunglasses you knew you saw
in the mussel shells of the sand
and the shells became lenses
as we looked for lenses
and they did become pearl eyes
and they did become chipmunk bellies
and you cleaned the sunglasses in the tide
and put them on your face
and we now admire the perfection
of this found object
the harmony of face and tool
the octaves of shape.

We found a hypodermic needle
without its needle.
We buried it in the sand.
We slept and burned on the sand.

THE LANGUAGE OF THE ENSLAVED

It could have been worse.
It is better than it could have been.
The language of the enslaved.

We know exactly who we want
as we watch the moon rise through the summer trees
and we figure God comes broken like this,
shards of light through the mess of line,
strobing, going point, going beam,
fighting to become full and bare.
And then he is there, underwhelming.

I went to São Paulo to be with her
to finally sacrifice myself
but she had mostly forgotten me,
taking selfies at the cafe downtown.
I lived in a district covered in human shit.
She told me it was very dangerous
and shrugged when we separated
at the end of the slow escalator.

In Santiago it had been the answer
and she hugged me where the notes to God
were strung on a wire
near the chapel
where I saw us married in white,
the city below, under the orange dust.
She reached out to me at the club
where the big fat men
waited for the pressure of small women
against the bar.
She would not kiss me near her hostel.
She was soft with me in the park.
We spoke in a terrible Spanish.
I maybe got the singer pregnant.

The hole could be a portal.
Evolution could be sweeping you off the table.
I stood in Puerto Natales and she was gone.
I stood in the parhelion country and she was gone.

The Fires

I am on the floor and she is gone.
I will huff sugar and swim in sedate creek.
I will entwine myself with piano wire.
I will break the doorhandles off all these sedans.
We will live in the apartment with tropical birds.
Do you remember when we went into the warm mud?

DO YOU DO GLASS?

I had to tell a methhead the sun was bigger than the earth.
What? But the earth is so massive.
I know. I know. It's hard to believe.
How can that be?
I don't know. I haven't done the research myself.
But that's what I hear.
Wow.
I know. And not just a little bit bigger
not a golfball and a grapefruit
but a pupil and a mansion.

She asked me if I did glass.
I didn't, but it seemed like a good night to start.
We smoked weed instead, by her open window,
in the night of the city wind through the fire escape.
She said I was such a stoner
but I wasn't that either.
We kissed until we were both tired.
I slept on the couch
and she on the bed
in the studio apartment
on the Upper West Side.
We lay and stared at a common ceiling
and I conveyed the fact I had learned
but I no longer believe myself.
I am only a receiver and a transmitter.
I am only an impoverished repeater.
Now I believe I am that which
hears of the earth and the sun
and hears the earth is smaller than the sun
and I say the earth is smaller than the sun
to a woman who asked
Do you do glass?

BRAINLASH IS REAL

Hiding deep in summer
adding seltzer to the wine.
Hiding from the age and my own age
and what can no longer be done.
She blinked and said the escaped eyelash
had been sucked behind her eye
and gone into her brain.
I said maybe you'll dream of it.
She said maybe I'll forever see it
like a black scratch on the lens.
She laughed and laughed
and she stopped and she laughed.
She did dream of it.
Brainlash is real.

THE COMICBOOK SHOP

Always in some stage of healing
and my dad had a comicbook shop
in a haunted hotel.
Now the world is a haunted hotel
and I try to make
pamphlets of coherence.
There is never a reason
to keep looking for a reason
when looking is really waiting
and waiting is hoping
and hoping is the business of the fool.
The west turns to the Tao.
The east turns to Michael Jordan.

You will meet someone new to cure you of your vision.
To see you have a different concern
a different obsession.
They have come upon a different theme of details
but our vision is all we have.
We will not be cured. We cannot be.
Conquerors are remembered,
prophets, messiahs.
We are what we see
though not really. We are what we remember.
But not that. We are who keeps awakening.
We are what is incurable.

END USER / ULTRA PURE

Delicious packets of verbiage
for the outofwork gospel singer
kicking a tinsel halo under
the marquee now a home for nest.
Champagne bottle on the piano
in the frigid Queens apartment
with the summerbridge under glass
and the drawer of summerknives.

A scattering of tickets on the starred sidewalk
and a Caribbean wind comes through
as an escaped memory.
We are waiting for that which justifies our waiting,
almoners knitting deathcap
for a variety of wheezing accountants
at the hospice you hope to implode
when you clickfinish the white
and offwhite Rubik's cube.

Love requires focus
and will these cement ramps ever end.
Sunrise over sweating walls
and there are destroyed grocery stores
in the narrative of that man
and there are gumwads
and there are blackened stencils
and there are beery dragoons
riding old mops and brooms
in closets used for e-cig breaks.
We learn to politely say:
You are screwing me.

Back when I used to pet books,
back when we were broken up
and having way better sex,
can we stand in our toppling kitchens
and say it's all a mess.
The touch of a stranger is more profound.
Fear will deepen you, it will instruct you,
it will make you interesting,

she looked at me from the table
with eyes that had been through the assault
she pet my belly
she squeezed my unfit arms.
Mushroom cloud on the dresser top.

When the one material does become granular
and each grain contains itself and all others
our friendships will lose their eroticism
and we will chew sandwiches, sadly,
and we will start doing pushups again,
dont tempt me, dont bet against me,
the home garbage is fermenting
so we can drink of it
and bear the next wedding.

Yes Alan we did die long ago
and your entry ticket is still with you
and you sent me a photo of it:
5meoAMT skull and crossbones label.
Death is final. End user.
Guaranteed to meet or exceed
the specifications
on this label.
Ultra pure. 99.5+%

THE SHELLS

Marshalling thoughts
and pulling cubes from pyrite.
Heaven is parsed out in moments,
hell in decades.

When hell is remembered
it is usually diminished.
When heaven is remembered
it usually expands.
Not always.
But that's your problem.
You are a problem.
I am standing right here
right next to you
and you are bothering me.
Stop talking to me.
I started this but stop.

My little stethoscope
in the lot of things that cannot be repaired.
We could drive to where the wind does end.
We could run through the aisles
of that abandoned arcade
among the tilted signs
of the seaside empire.
Remember a breakfast with Dad
in a long hall
in a hot ocean morning
each table glare a cutter.
The wind will transfer you
to Vietnam rails
and the lavender curtains
of a passing train.
A deep cubic rise of autumn.

We are constantly called and always abandoned.
Made hot, made lonesome,
new people shrieking in the walls of water
and a golden cloud breaks over the boardwalk
where a woman says It's a white girl summer.

Bones and feathers on the sharp rocks
where a soft knife could remove the small jungle
and there is another folded napkin in plastic
as another mom fights cancer in a stuffy room
and did the Mandan really have white hair
and Alan says the subtext of life is ominous.
We hear echoes but never the voice.
We break into hotel pools.

This is not my home.
I do not belong here.
I want to leave.
What are you talking about?
We are not in the same place.
You are going on and on
about a world that is not my life.
You are a magus of information
but you tell me nothing.
I will vomit on you again.
I am poisoned here
I am kept from my true family
I am bound and I am sick
from the need for food
from the maniacal webbing of needs
I will not count for you
I do not see your line, your work of arc
There is only one division
and it is the line that brought me here
that made me here and not there
It is not a gift
It is not a privilege
You are a propagandist
You work for the distortion
Do not you dare tell me about the past
Do not you dare tell me about the future
In the future waits my freedom
In the past sleeps my freedom
I am surrounded atemporal by freedom
There are great hammocks waiting for me
Here there is only clawing
Here there is only longing
Here every freedom breeds a disease

The Fires

Here there is a cascade of virtuals
Here you look across for the enemy
when the enemy is above
when the enemy is below
when the enemy is inside
when the enemy is the stalker in your dreams
and it is the fact of dreaming
and it is the being of being
and it is something wrong
when everything is wrong
a tournament of specters
a total spectrum of poisons
a vast bland startlement
a movement tease
in voluptuous weathers
where the clouds are stacked
in banded fevers of white and yellow
and you rub her long brown belly
as she flowers her lips
and you walk in honest to god alleys
and pass men huddled below the corner trees
of a bank hardware parking lot.

Throw it up so black my departed friend,
through it up and put yourself against the harrowing sky.
Sway to the music of robotic ancients
in the field cut by the red viaduct.
Your arms up against the downed
and very near the drownedlands
Your lids dropped
Your navel regrowing its fair tube
to a new nurture
to a new womb
to the original egg
o dear one o hindi for dear
we are not long for these shallows cement
for these speckled puddles
for these calligraphic sprays of white paint and bird feces
We are not long and we are never here
and we are loved by a language we are learning
and it is a loss of the shells of the hidden
prison
crystalline.

WE DREAM OF MONGOLIA

Red and blue sirens through the windows we steamed
and a decorated cave of monks waiting for the return of the king
worlds break through
and you stare at me
and I was a herd grazing on your leg
and you are soaked through
and we are simple beings
full of Mediterranean food
and sweating wine from the unbalanced table
and hearing the warm genius of Tupelo Honey
we are drone and queen
and the rain sent us to our lips and our eyes
and faces and names tell the truth plain
and we dream of Mongolia
and I want to die on horseback under a ringing moon
and are you also sick of this world
and no one will save us
and we are exiles and we are wanderers
and God is two bright glimmers at the horizon
but he will not help
and we were near the UFO capital of the US
and you can take all the tea in China
and you wanted to go in the back
where my dad keeps a bin named HORROR
but I have a secret
and our secrets give us urges that give us cancer
and the genius was bullied
and the genius became an atheist
and the new vaccines mock the afflicted
and the man preferred the sea to the streets of Acapulco
and the weak did inherit all of this
long ago, far ago, so so long ago
and we are left to validate ourselves
and you were not raised with the words I love you
and we massage each other
two fearful yet two strong yet two normal
and there is baklava in the bag
for your mother and her innocence
and we wait amid bills for cures
and the horror does flood through the brief error

The Fires

and the open sunroof does put stars above us
and we are catalogues of stomach aches
and our friends are going insane
and I will not let myself live another year
because the bodymind conspires
against the very self it creates
and maybe it was ball lightning
and God sees through the eyes of each god
and you give me the air plant I forgot you gave me
and a box of coconut water
and I fall asleep and I dream and I do not remember my dreams
and who in this mistake will keep your secrets
and the confused mind does fail the beautiful body
and no one will be spared
and he makes a fool of us all
in our contents that have come too late
in our entrepreneurial fallout
and the world is too small for our desires
and he squeezes so we sing
and wail into canyons of marbled rock
and on ledge of conglomerate granite
and he does not care for any of us
and the scales are always balanced
and he has made steel sharkmouth for wolves
and we stoop through our rounds
and the way is indeed narrow
and we see the hospitals where we will daze
and work is our lot
and toil is our lot
and we quickly tire of learning
because the lesson is always pain
and we have found each other here
and we fail to make each other healed
and will you put orange with the pasta
and it goes, it goes on,
and does true fear burn in your belly
like a mound of chilies
and I want to be good to you
but we never know how
because there has been so much good
but not enough.

BECOMING WHALE

The machine song of whales
and the ocean itself is a sound
and this day is more normal
and fast incomplete.
A trail of blood at the supermarket
reveals itself to be
a bad route of sovereign cherries.

If I see my reflection one more time
I am going to punish what is reflected.
I want pure navigation. I want less effort.
He was so perfect he died at twentyeight,
a neongreen spider, tiny, rested on his black lapel.
We pit our versions of luck against each other
over the red waters of the valley mountains.
He was fantastic and gleaming
and maybe his twentyeight
is your
ninetythree.

She asked me if I was a romantic.
Maybe once. But not twice.
You start thinking about benefits.
You start thinking it is better
to do less than more,
the world a nest of idiot hands.
They claw and scratch and shake
and they never touch what it is
they are fighting toward.
Buy yourself a rose.
I wish I was and I still am,
just in different ways.

Old phonebook of failures
in every shattered phone booth
in every southwest corner
of every garbled lot.
The landlord sits in his sunset office
that is more a stationery museum
and he is moaning into the dictaphone

he is moaning and he is clacking
he is becoming a forever machine
finally perfect and finally smooth
and the air is a water of bliss
above the delicate flesh of sound
and he is tired and he is unloved
and he is a son without a daughter
and he is a eunuch father in the machine progress
and he is trying to reach the logical summit of machine progress
and he is trying to become whale.

YOU WILL LOVE ME

You will love me.
You will turn your eyes to me
in the morning sun we come to agree
is very good and very new.
You will fit into the profile of my body
like the first self that contains
the secret of the building
of the second self, the self now entire.

You will love me and you will tell me.
You will track the edges of my temples
and tell me that I have been true,
that I have been just.
You will hand me a paper cup
of steaming black americano.
You will keep things I say
in one of those notebooks you carry.
You will shake your head and laugh
at my regular brilliance.
You will consider yourself lucky
in the bed of a Swiss hotel.
You will say that no one else compares.

You will see my inexplicable grief
and you will massage the cords of my strength.
You will go energetic
when we meet on flowered patios.
You will laugh and hook your arm
around my neck
and offer me water
from your tall cool glass.

You will collect my nails and hair
when I attain the rainbow body
and shower the golden hills of Tuscany.
You will dream of me, and sex with me,
and you will miss me
when I leave to impress you
with another adventure.

You will prank me, you will stop me
from disappearing
into the rug and into the floor.
You will lead me to the hammock
and to shade and ripe tomatoes.
You will tell me that the world is good
and you will put my finger inside you
and you will bite your own lip
as the humidity finally breaks
in a crush of déjà vu and citrus.

RUNNING BEARS

There are blue crystals in the heart of a strawberry.
She gave me a black mulberry
on the path to the distant cemetery
and we kissed in what I called weeds.
Her eyes pulse when she talks.
She did not care for Indonesia.
There is a kind of love that grows so slow
but is huge in two weeks,
her toenails painted my favorite blue.

She becomes a child and she becomes
a sardonic adult. We peel the pink armor
from the lychee. How long must we hear
our own voices out in the firefly grass.
Developments and cubic growth
and men discussing therapy in the water
of the high mountain reservoir,
a floating tree and the persistence
of black and red ants
on the rock dusted by pastel chalk,
the serenity of a hovering
raptor over a green forest barely
interrupted by our silver effort.
There is haze, there is the echo
of the rope of the flag.
A bubbly Vietnam vet
saying vets are tough
and could bite the ass off
a running bear.

THE BEAST

On the branch there are two black hats and two black coats.
Shadow Lee told us to put the money in escrow.
You will dream about her dressed in red silk,
folding silkpaper into boxes and smashing them flat.
I wonder if I was hoping the car would crash,
blasting metal, and I remember certain polar drunks
only because I hallucinated rain.

What do I hope to gain from suicide?
Nothing. I expect nothing.
Expectations do not belong here.
But I do expect a shift, a change.
I do not think the totality
has the capacity to decrease suffering
so I expect a different kind of suffering
which can be a temporary decrease
of this suffering, before the genius of its depth
is illuminated
with the geometrical flare
of fresh pain.
Eternity is a long time.
We have nowhere to go.

Your knowledge of pleasure has expanded
to allow the full number of its opposite.
Most humans enter screaming
and soon hope for flat bellies
and soon hunt the allfire for the hatch.
Where will we go? No one will miss us.
Our presence activates the field.
Janet Craig is an African plant.
Dad is increasingly annoying.
Brothers move to Albany
to split their surnames with their wives.
Do animals see humans as one undying beast
walking through the trees,
trailing mist, honing its tools,
perfecting its meals.
They are always crooning.
They are usually wailing.

An elder is seated at a wooden table
and his forefinger runs the surface
to describe the lines
of a ritual designed
to eradicate the work of the doppelgänger.

The Fires

BATHE IN HER LONG HAIR

You must think of new compliments
so you can bathe in her long hair
so you squint against her widening eyes
so you can cut this haunting and leave it behind.
If she does not love me, if she will not love me,
I will continue the transgression of lesser tones
I will bother the world in dustridden walks
I will not like who I was to become this
and I will have to start all over again
to feel the same again
to array stupid consolations
on the morning sill
in the morning of sky and crow.
Effort is required and demanded.
Effort is needed for the maintenance
and effort needed for the building
and is not everything a type of work,
sloth the negative rain, sloth the void drop,
can we not just lie and nap
under that canopy of palms,
what is enough for your love
for your superior attention, I can smell you,
I wonder who you really want
I wonder who has attained you by the easiness
of their being and I wonder if you can read
my nonspecific and general exhaustion
the readiness of my hands to release
the quickness of my immobility
just lie with me on this red felt
secluded from the roundabout of guards,
I am good at most times,
yet yes I am old yet yes I am flawed
and so you and so us all
turning and blind and
from our magicbox a cloud will rise,
no one long convinced,
no one less the wise.

THE REVERSE TOWER

The horses wild and green
on the streets of Olinda
jaw garbage
and men make carts of this food
and attach themselves
to the horses.

The stone well. The reverse tower.
It gets hotter after it rains, fishermen
standing on the strip of rock
and moss. It looks like a fallen tree
in the shallows, and they are black
against the sky.

She used to dream of a bull
and her grandmother poured vinegar
into the fresh chickenblood.
Janitors on rollerblades. Guards
on segues. A politician can break
the country.

Do you know what you're doing?
Fumbling, freezing fingers
in tropical climate, in heavy haze.
She smirks, she's waiting for a call
from a firm.
The struggle of a yellow butterfly,
or is it a moth,
stirred against the tan condominium.
It is so quiet here.

THE SIXTY CLOCKS

In the room of sixty clocks each clock is at a separate second
so the striking of the hour falls in a cascade.
In the air I found a hidden mausoleum
arrayed in a cube of cubes
the lines tight and shimmering
and if you touch a cube
that cube will grow
and it will open
like the drawer of a filing cabinet
and a tiny body will be there, face like napping cat.
I want to say metallic tongues.

The young man has come to be
and always was
the least exciting demographic.
So advertise accordingly.
Out on the roof with your hand and arm
raised as your only antenna
you will receive mystic jargon
you will go pure horror
at the meld of east and west.

Blacklace witch on her dollarstore broom
she gonna fall when she hits that moon.

Supernatural orders bogart the magnetized lexicon.
They have commandeered the power words.
The solar body will attain the orgasmic wisdom.
Fathers and mothers and ghosts and winds
and the everpresent circle, the outofbody eye.
The adept descends to his basement of pillars.
Attainment near, common attainment beer.
Breaking sheets of glass to make ultimate puzzles.

Frost medallions on the past pride of brick lords.
Gold medallions on the past brides of equine hordes.
Hold me, transport me on a great insect
down the long avenue of intense boutique
down the water channel that allows the viewing
of the contours of every rock

in its provisional bed I am drifting,
I am dreaming of a now
1° better, for I have learned the carpet coat of greed.

THE DEATHBED

Your brain needs a colonoscopy,
he said. Once. And now he is here.
Laid out on the deck in the sun.
Laid out on dense white foam.
When his eyes are open gates
he begins to speak again,
he even smokes, he asks for black coffee.
He asks for amaretto
rich pasta
red steak
the ass of a twentysomething.

You are not alone, he says,
but you really are alone.
You are alone with your pain.
You are alone with your joy.
Your memories are not real
but they are all that you have
and they are often
the best method of suicide.
You are alone with the width
of your perception
of your experience
which will indeed
make less sense
as long life insists on removing
everything you come to
stand upon
everything you come to
clutch.
God is real
but not all the time
and It will not be heard
when you need It most
but It will occasionally
apologize
and hand you an excuse:
It is a complicated
universe. So
Bring me iced water.

Bring me a decent red.
Bring me a brace and bit
for my third eye.
Bring me her lips
when she was a bartender
and twentyfive.

He is asleep again.
The dunes are blue
and the dunes of his palms
are blue
and I am blue
but the sky is—

Do not say it is red,
he says,
maybe it is a slice
of falcon liver.
Do not succumb
to the weak
impressions of others.
Get blown in Cusco
and make straight decisions
and if you put ice
into a strong liquor
I will call the cubes
training wheels.
Fuck and die.
Eat butter and die.
With forefinger out
admire her hips
and die.
All flows, they were right
about that.
And all changes,
they were right about that too.
But you can be
the only one
who believes it.
You can be
a hidden warrior.
I have left a manual
on this very thing

in the Turkish chest
of the south corner bedroom.
The first page
is the mandala of initiation.
It appears to be
a harmless circular design
but it is a doorway.

By staring yourself
into the frontier of
this eternal
bleak substance
you will come to see the truth
of these trials and these sessions
You will drink of the sadness
from the bottomless well
and you will drink from a standard
cup, cracked and brown
You will shine apples
and drink champagne like a blade
and you will punch hard and fast
You will know the tiered whispers
and you will put footprints
into the dust of the road
You will not like what you find
but you will be beyond
the cult of favor
You will cross kisseyed mothers
and you will oil their caesarean scars
You will count silver in dry rooms
and you will polish the bottles
of lanky bartenders
from the mountains
You will becry the great exhaustion
and the work of dedicated immigrants
in seeping and spoiled kingdoms
You will admire the serration of wrappers
and you will understand my poisonous charms
You will know that every face
reveals the truth of its wearer
You will know that the obvious
is hard come by

in this vale of energy and destitute hour
and you will see the ongoing emptiness
of every gesture and of every word
You will astonish your own cruelty
and you will pull the hair
of favorite daughters
and you will curse
the languid circling
of sons who still wipe
breastmilk from their twisted
bemused grins
You will hear the spew of statistic
and will be tasked by precise historians
as the maps become revelatory
as the swarms are given definite colors
and you will offend the sacrosanct
in bedroom musings
that become massive geometry
on distant city bridges
the world only a receptacle
the world a story
the world the summation of your memory
the world a dream merrily
and you will weep less for the children
and you will weep less for the abused
and you will laugh at the wisdom of the people
as the compost turns
as the meat is exchanged
from plate to plate
on the always balanced scales
as AI scientists become
monotone prophets
nothing lost nothing gained nothing made
as you write songs in your sleep
only to lose the love
of every coppered woman
in every foreign street
of dick pills and knockoff jeans
only to wander the expanse and waste
of the only path
mountains rising in only your eye
You will know the sober laughter of the sage

The Fires

and you will step aside from the fast train
of present morality
and you will dine on rare blood
encircled by telepathic cats
in beaten Caribbean tinrooms
and you will speak to harmonic reflections
in the jungle grown
from the memory extract
of what a forest is
and the chambers of a pomegranate
and you will treat her lap like an altar
and you will watch big men
ride wheeled speakers
on suburban streets
and you will see my surrender
to the confounding madness
of that which is
and you will know my weeping
equal to laughter
as outofplace parrots
land outside your window
as you know
we are the work of a vast spirit
and yes that is true too,
even though it is wrong, the true kind,
and you will become the great enemy
by your own vacancy and immunity
and when you die the death of the hero
you will blink
and you will be staring
at the mandala on the page
in a room blessed by crossbreeze
as I am about to blink
and stand in a room
blessed
by crossbreeze.

FOCUS

Focus.
Detest. Thimbles of borrowed rain,
broken beltloops. Rain pressing
down on the summer pollen.
Who is the most recent
insane. Pyramid mysteries, fear of
earwax, the increasing audacity of VR.

Focus.
Elaborate programs to avoid incest.
Trees grow from skull mouths,
from skull eyes, the mundane
messages of the divine.
Please locate your career
in the dark, please tell me
if suffering is worth it.
Palms cooling cups of hot water.
Coupons on the reverse of receipts.
You remind me of someone I once
wanted, dashboard warnings
keep me alight. In your pocket
collections of presidential teeth.

Focus.
In scars hidden the wordless data
of Sirius transmissions. Men's rights
activists climbing northeastern trees,
pied piper in the lined fans of a gingko.
Chunks of hamburger in hotdog buns
and the solemn declaration of Bingo.
I'm not winning, seven hundred years,
eight billion, we are running out of money
and the uses of money and the
use of use, what is it, what goes there,
what has been
thrown against the air, the air
of nursing homes where plastic
is never quite clean.

Focus.
Amass sexual opportunity. Invite
me over. Carvings in your favorite window
so you never forget me, shoeboxes
of the toys you wanted as a child.
Underlining underlines
and waiting for the right word. Pull the stage
like you would a rug, mouth full of
dandelion leaves and maple wine.
The scraping of flattop grills,
the sunglasses of the rowdy cobb master.
Brother, what strange medicine is this?

Focus.
We meet each other in the great yawn
before the little belch, Shadow Lee
laughing all the way down Ryerson Street.
Necklace of twine, circle of red yolks.
Leaning fathers give direct lessons
to children already tending hate like
a long line of bonsai. Do not enter my dream,
the woodgrain will become currents.
Do not enter my home,
the drinks will become detergent.
If I could see a wolf every day things
would be so much better. We have
lost the grip we never had, we will
no longer go to Arby's with Omar,
the funk compilation tapes
have been lost to the vaquero of objects.
Dipped fingers in pancake batter
remembered on the whitest of deathbeds
below a Croatian sky, so dry, when I say Focus
you say On what.

AT LAST WE ARE STRANGERS

At last we are strangers.
Our friends no longer call us
for joyride and for helium release
off skeletal redbridges,
we miss the elastic lips
of the woman who visited
so brown in jean cutoffs.

We are become deep
but we are not profound
but we are still surprised
we think children wont die
we cower with 2 liters of cola
on the curb of interstellar gem.

A black thread through one ear
and out the other, did you know
you turn the earth as you walk.
Dad keeps marbled halvah in the fridge
and eats it with a spoon, saying
Open the steeple and see all the

We will be shot in the street
because people are shot in the street.
There's simply no one else to shoot.
We use appropriated yoyo string
to make connections in real time
and real space, cardoor to face.
He loves me once, she loves me not,
and she's eight times a lady.
Do we want bloated heroes to die.
Do we really believe in the basic goodness
mentioned by Chögyam Trungpa.

Are we remembered by less.
Have we lost our mojo.
If there is a groove,
how do we get it back.
Men still fear the factory toll.
Women still fear riders on the road.

We are become sad strangers
dropped in the ornery beleaguerment
of metropolitan hustle.
We wear little hats
and rebel against our tricycles
but we still ring the bells.
We are prodded into love
and starved into business
and we only dream about the tree of lions
once.

THE CELIBATE WOMEN OF NEW JERSEY

Apes pawing in the barren field
looking for jewel, looking for hard color,
looking for seventeen eyelashes.
Bodies stacked behind the last wall of the rock cabin.
Somewhere there are shelves with canisters
of lethal gas. Muted in the stainedglass strata
of hypnoses. Donut coffee, hands jabbing theses,
people waiting for their daily fix of attention.
A deck of cards with reasons for carrying on.
Shuffle, pull, repeat, waiting for the light to change.

The celibate women of New Jersey
and a man with beautiful eyes
saying how waiting for his wife
changed his life.
You inhale in the morning bedroom
the dust like smoke
and turn your hands clockwise
and you summon the current state
of reality. Fiat lux, skateboard trucks,
everything in its right place, indentation
for the marble, plug for the outlet,
the more obscure the wiser.
Speak with your actions,
splayed out in aisles of cacophony
and rants of Bach things go
on but not definitely for the better.
After orgasm hear the highway ghost.
You have perfected your bow
before the secret king
and his white cloak
of silk and gold filigree
(one drop of blood).

MILK SNAKE

I fell in the woods and almost fell in the water
and the people in the woods and the water saw it
but there was no embarrassment.
How far we can come.
Let the sun paint your back red
in the red pool of the bright falls
because there is a rusted turbine in the woods
and graffiti over it that says Turnbine.

Her smell made me want to breed
on that soft bed in the loft of the rental.
I called it a pheromone attack.
She was tall and black with a flowing confidence.
She said she had a relaxed mind.
I never saw her again.
I guess she did not smell
the sweet possibility of generations.

Milk snake on the rock, like waves on the log,
a small blackbear fast across the road
and the man in the mask is from Tibet.
We are far from home and we are never home.
There are corners unknown
where the unknown festers.
Compassion is more a mythic city
than some backyard garden.

If I were looking for discord violence
dismay confusion hatred sorrow regret
longing pleasure quotes and candy
this is just the place I would come.

YOUR STUPID MOTHER LOVED YOU

Your stupid mother loved you.
She should not have had children
but she had you. She cut strawberries
and placed them in cream. She sewed thread
to the end of the belt
of your football pants
so she could pull the belt
through the secret waistline tunnel
allowing the belt and pants
to actually work
while the other kids
looked insane and disheveled,
the belts crooked and barely attached
and really, totally, pointless.

Her mother was Italian and kept in asylums
when she was not weeping in the living room
when she was not making a bowl of pasta
when she was not shuffling through chores.
I don't know. I never met her.
Your mother wanted to make a better family
and maybe promised herself
to never go insane.
The coffee is brewing. She is going to work.
The coroner's office she helped to build
gave her a weird trophy.

She was not the best and she was not the worst
but she was pretty good
and she pushed you into The Bronx.
(I can't imagine they still put babyfeet
in pads of ink.) She was once thin.
She was once divorced. Who are these makers?
We smiled together in a pile of leaves.

She told me I needed a job
and she told me she got me a job.
I would ask for a pack of Newports
at the gas stations and convenience stores
of the river valley. I was twelve.

The Fires

Whoever sold the smoke was fined.
One clerk knew the score
and ran into the parking lot
screaming
as me and the hot interns
sped away
in a car
laughing.
Your mother died from cigarettes.

THE AIRSTREAM

Beware of the miracle worker that lives in the Airstream
out by the marsh and the abandoned railroad
for he healed the mechanic and his yard of relics
and he makes guitar rituals under every full moon.

Is it still the land of canoe and weeping willow
hung over electric wire. Is that house still haunted
in Savannah, the drummer obsessive
watching Ren and Stimpy videocassettes.
In Chattanooga we tried to sleep
in the endless house
as the livingroom pitbulls
made us believe
in ghost after ghost.

There were wet open houses in Gainesville,
big walls of black windowscreen,
and there were clean Target aisles
all over the midwest. Yes there are still fireflies
in our vaulted trees, there are still Christian pamphlets.
You can still see fresh graffiti
between the graveyard and the faded road
on the walls of the cement tunnel.

I once saw him covered in ladybugs.
He closed his mouth. He closed his eyes.
He had attained a second body.
When they were on him they looked dead.
They left him in one burst.
The interior of the Airstream was so neat
it did something to my mind.
Amtrak coffee is a truth serum
and fat men will snore in suspenders.

Is there a place with monks and poets in the hills.
Is there still a glowing box in the navel of the forest.
Do you still watch the trees for hiding bums
and do they still look for robin eggs.
Did I really lose my virginity in Asheville
and did she grind against me above the white river.

The Fires

You can still see a coyote among the graves of the salesian.
You still believe in roaming archers.

Do college dropouts still eat from cans of beans
and can you still flip through a directory of farms
and work for the families of famous rock stars.
When you think of Italy do you still picture weathered hands
opening a jar in a windblown kitchen.

We still dream of marquees in clear Colorado towns.
I am still thinking of moving to Portland, Maine.
I still want to press aloe into her cooking skin
in a lazy bedroom in Miami (reggaeton, mango).
The miracle worker had a name for every deer
and he always proffered a cold Coors Light
though I never saw him drink
anything but creek water.

COLD CANS OF SELTZER

That space by her elbow that felt like marshmallow
or the drone dimension made by the garbage truck
out on the road that divides the blackdirt fields.
She forgot we had a date and the wifi guru laughs:
There will not actually be
a flying white horse
at the end of Kali Yuga.

We battle growth with sponges
and we listen to drunk monks talk about drala.
We tell each other about the killer on the loose
who left an abducted girl at a gas station
near Paterson, New Jersey.
Somehow, that is the saddest part.
As long as the seltzer is canned and cold
we figure we can make it.

Do not let your friends smoke too much weed
and do not neglect the importance of sleep.
You cannot afford expensive things
but if you buy a cheap thing
you will need to buy two more.
The lazy man does twice the work,
she told me, before she married that carpenter.
I was the reliable dishwasher
who broke her favorite cup.

Children still make :) with chalk
and if you put your ear
to the opening of the gas tank
you can hear the sound of the highway.
We are sick of cleaning.
We have always sensed something wrong.
Appreciating this world
takes maniacal vigilance
and deer hearts of amnesia,
it takes a strong hypnosis
it has been kind enough to offer
among toothpick and mint
at the Vietnamese restaurant,

it takes a father
smoking forever
in a rusted Nissan.
We will not sleep on invisible floors
among the crowns of trees
watching pearlwhite monkeys
with daphneblue eyes.
We are so tired of ourselves
and even the best versions
of ourselves
and no Buddhist will save us,
no ornate Celtic letter,
no lover, no friend,
you will go cancer along the metro line
with a small collection of bookmarks,
you will chew coffeegrinds
and imagine giving CPR
to the third dead chipmunk today.
It is no one's fault, you say,
it is no one's fault.

THE PHONE BOOTH IN THE ONION FIELDS

The rice boiling like angry salmon
and in the night there is a matrix of eyes.
Connect any to any and each to each
| node |village |lamppost|| |
to make the story of your life in syrupy light.

First memory:
dry taste of the deckwood make feet curl.
The hyphens that make the strings in bass tablature
are perforations on the snowground. Do not run
from the whim of Celsius, has anyone
examined the back of Lincoln's head
on Mount Rushmore? I live in the cavity
repeating fourscore, Darwin steeping
that same damn xícara of tea. Walk in the forest
but the flowers throw bleachwipes.
When the blinds are tight the strings are lousy
bundles of DNA.

The Chilean prostitutes sit like a jury
waiting to read the bank receipt folded
in your fifth pocket, but you want to describe
the epiphany of ten bodies
in Mexico,
white flags
at the end of the roll of toilet paper.

There is a phone booth in the onion fields
that will ring if you stop biting your nails,
shamans in dungarees commiserating
over the first refills of coffee, along the counter,
on the last day of the diner.
My friends had access to the music school
and clattered the instruments
while asking their pupils to dilate
in the night of the green, the yellow, the red.

REDSHIFT

Cherry cordial and redshift,
the universe is vast and pleading,
blood blister and strawberry milk,
crimsonblack firstfruit, spherical,
ripe, the moon is losing blush.

The horizon between her legs
is pink and clean and plunge
your hands into the feathered water.
Veins of saffron at the edge of suburbia.
Honeycrisp apple but the taste of pear,
the desert of burnt sand and paprika,
as Mercury begins to strobe
in the vermilion carpet of dawn sleep.

THE PROMISED LAND

Paradise is always behind us,
or it's a sunshower in Recife,
right now. Broken white lines.
God is a thrower of plagues.
There were moments for the Israelites
when desert freedom
was worse
than desert bondage.
And where are we now?
The slave project, the wilderness,
or the promised land.

Pressed back to the earth
when we begin to hover and fly,
our skin marked, our stores gutted.
Barbed words from strangers.
We are trained in a series of disasters.
We learn that pain hurts
and works
as a gravel path
for more pain.
I'm sorry, I have to use your bathroom
right now.

The path is too narrow, a blank rope
soaked in ether, bending rainbow
above vintage flames.
How you remake
your mind
is made by your mind
already made.
Anyway, it feels that way.

Ye made us and ye made us flawed.
Ye made us incapable of protocol.
Ye made us dumbfound, ye made us
stiffnecked, the punishment
so fixed
it has made
the idea of itself.

Save us. Save us from the thought
of being saved.
Save us from the wrought,
save us from the wicked,
ye have put your holed finger
into the water
but ye have not made
the waves.

THE FASCINATION

Finite and infinite plasma, melt
backward to the first and last point,
is the real reach ever-outward
and ever-inward. And are those two
directions the same.

Golden rib to golden hip.
In the night the wind will carry
the smell of fried food, it will lift
the moon to a pill. A cascade
of fake white orchids. When I get a disease,
the world gets one.

Cadenza tells me to go home, the age
of quarantines has begun, or,
it starts again, death still
the fascination.

WE WONT

We wont to meet again.
Bright messy words from the speakers
mounted on a passing car. Selling.
Warning.
Mango. Pandemic.
Watch the rope of water
leave the vessel.

A man on the ground and blood from his head,
one sandal gone. The man beside him,
crouched, is the seller of grilled cheese,
a vendor of the beach, the waves behind them,
and his white smock
and his black glasses
make him look like a child...
Yellow grass about the tennis court,
straight sunlight
between the high rises.

ALABASTER

Put your finger inside and think of me.
Take it out and lick it and
think of me. Black wallpaper on the roof.
Clear plastic on the roof
of the refrigerator. Alabaster,

At The Drive-In. Those stuffy rooms
making dust that lands on the turntable,
the room a cornered moon of dust,
our houses only makers of dust.
Groves of plastic, narrow canyons.
Vodka bottle in a sheath of frost.
Marijuana ash, plastic bag.
Is there anything worse than a videocassette
viewed in the middle of the day.
The curtains block the judgmental eye,
the snow outside, it holds black rocks.

She mouths a Shakira song
but there is no sound, so just her tongue
licking the space
before the lens.

THE HOUSE OF FIVE SISTERS

The house of five sisters and the orgy of citrus.
Moses running between the Israelites and God.
There is always some poor mediator, out in the waste,
she texted me in the morning:
Why are lucky people so dumb?

Sprinkleth the tap water on your immigration dreams,
young one, working so hard at the men's suit store
in the mall, strong liquid kept in vials
and those vials in socks, there is so much stuff,
and Italy is on lockdown, my friend walking there again
to mend his sciatica. She is a spiritist now and a whore
in a past life, which is why she loved
Montmartre.

THE OFFENDED SORCERER

The curse works backwards and forwards
and at 45 I met the sorcerer I offended.
My friend said reading is baroque, while virtual reality
reaches for the reality we are already in, the flawed space,
the land of blemish. VR so real... but can it blow you?
Press the plunger for the cleaner.

The tides of misfortune, invisible but painfilled,
the language of the Bible will increase its massage
in a Boa Viagem bedroom, all the cold
trapped in the freezer, kids flattening cans
with their feet, a small boy adding his bag of milk
to your groceries at the silent store.
The belt does not move. The cashier almost nods.

Years will accumulate but nothing will pass.
Assorted defeats admitted to no one,
though you've gotten better at lists
and tax payments. The masses unmoved
or is it just you in the material deluge,
though things are losing their dimensions,
the world forming your ephemera and soul
as it crushes, infests your body. Death is when
the timer goes off. Maximum discomfort,
too much life.

The curse had spread in every direction
and every possible direction, and he winked at me
after fish and chips, cold beer on the sidewalk.
So it finally makes sense, the itch and rash
time has given me, abrasive air, a parliament
of chattering ideas, an alphabet
of box inchoate. The alchemists had it right:
existence is a fire.

40

The drama of escaping energy, opposites retract.
Impossible scores on defeated arcade games, tucked away
in the corner of a mall built on swamp. Fantasies of sleep
will come to you, as you turn your car around the hospital
lanced with light. Somewhere between the elevators
there are sharks in the water.

The fan and the refrigerator will harmonize, theorize.
I pictured sweaty dark chapels but they dance
under fluorescence, in outfits white, clapping,
swinging, drinking ayahuasca. Can we influence anything,
hands folded
on a belly groaning: what is the mind horizon.

Panels of Tarot laid on the bathroom walls, ashflake
and ashpowder, a fortieth birthday—who
would celebrate such a thing?

SPECTACULAR VELOCITY

Baroque nests falling like dominoes you must
be sure to enter the password correctly.
We obey the line, we fill the rectangle
with rectangles, be mindful of the flame
pushed by the manufactured breeze.
In your hotbox. Your modern sweatlodge.

Framed portraits of jungle detritus. The cult
of a trainhopper, a man of the rails. How do
they always find the golden light. Perhaps
they live in the light and trust its bounty.

If you are not resourceful, ye are little in my sight.
Multiply, find yourself arrested and focused,
open skeletons wandering the shore harnessed
to huge balls of cans, they are ants. Shrug,
cross your arms, go sarcophagus.

THE TSAR BOMBA

It was not snow but pure ash
in the afterwhite of the sunyolk of the Tsar Bomba.
The people were gone, fast and deleted.
I walked in the supreme quiet.
The screams were inhaled by the amanhecer.
The troubles were simplified in the total blizzard.
I did see, by the fountain, two statues of powder,
arms upraised, mouths agape, eyes broken shields.
I did see, in the negative sky, one car aloft,
broken into pixels, black flame, nothing.
A thought could stir the radioactive down.
It was then I saw the sandhill crane,
losing dust as it flew the dust, as it fought
the morning of tense gravities and ovoid storm.
The beat of wings like footsteps in pulverized chalk.
Its red eyes were imagistic echoes of the world eater.
In its claws was the orphic egg, the black serpent
a nascent ladder round the paleblue shell.
I walked beneath the halved arch.
I passed the blank hydrant, the child sarcophagus.
It was then I saw the lamassu in the flaking street.
It stayed like a deer. It watched me. It made no track.
It was mute and observant in this gargantuan tomb.
The iris was black and in the wings an iridescent effect.
No cloud from its mouth, the hoofs wet, oiled.
It began to pulse and shudder and the eyes flared.
In the brief night of a blink it found exit.
I was alone again in the magnificence.
I saw but would not touch a grapefruit,
blinding in the soft absence, a solar extract.
This was glass in the intestines and I passed it,
I refused to look back at it.
As I walked the drifts of a long arcade I saw the burning ones.
Their wings were solid liquidity and mesmeric.
Their song was a song remembered.
It was a concentrated language frequency
and a red thread through the spheric zone of my life.
They were made of a separate matter.
They were the most real in my accumulation of real.
The one hand was somewhere at hand.

The wheel of eyes was coming and it had arrived
and it had seen all and none and it had left.
The burning ones broke the bounds of movement,
they were in constant motion but did not blur,
appearing, flickering, behind my eyes, before them.
They rotated with bizarre circumference.
Their wings were the last vestige of the fire color.
Their eyes were mirrors and numbers and white diagram.
The holy song intensified until it vanished them.
I realized I was not cold and let go.
In this destitute womb and in this realm of gossamer
I was beginning to master my pace and
to warm in the glow without heat.
I was beginning to be blind and to see
that I was the new and fatal king,
the terminal and fading regent,
hovering between the walls of life and death
in the bounteous turning of the clock of law,
in the white shadow of the imminent throne.

The Fires

GOOD TIME COURT

Across from the building of bright windows.
No one lives there, people walk there, men drill there.
The ghost fragments are in the alley between.
Broken eighties clocks on the stripped mantel
and the field painting contains the world tree
where I was coated in stellar pollen by the man of blue dawn
and entered into the infinity whose coordinates
I am in the midst of making by learning.

Seven and five are key components.
One. Nine. I am drunk and splayed
saying the good times are behind us
and I grew up on Good Time Court
where the dogs ran, one with three legs strawcolored.
I would put water droplets to your dimples.
I would bash my face against the slum concrete.
I would roam Lisbon and I would scratch at her doorhandle
in the rotating blue chambers of the night.

The cherries are with the winter pastries,
the glaze with the milk reflection, the white almond.
The modem is a shrine on the strip before the microwave,
homeless man screaming You can do what you want
his face a medieval mask of minstrel inkmap and metal stud.
One song played since March and her face reminds me
of the two mothers with whom I never had a threesome.

The Essenes, the secret alphabet and frightened influencer.
Gig economics and bright candydrops on old tickertape.
Why fuck a part when you can fuck the whole thing.
Dreary, decadent, veering from benchmen in parks
becoming benchmen in parks, an echo can be static
and still and unborn in the sudden air, revived foliage,
the desperate origami of seedpaper, collected and awaiting
tragedy in halogen bunkers, the vessel prophecy filled by water,
drinking water and recounting every tap, tapping counter by counter,
praying to your weird for perfect starvation holes in bygone,
in study of plains, in tomahawk boyhood, in winded tristate,
a hand to sign in the bathroom mirror the name of the proper address,
the right language to learn so you have a distress to send
when you remember/make the location of home.

The visions have become Segalike, and useless, and sole memory,
vectors of the death chart, she wants to tuck me in,
we're all tired, it's not going to be okay,
drink this, don't bruise the gin, it is, it will not, just be, it will not,
it is night and a baby is being made one story down,
another one to imprison, another one to reprimand,
who will exact revenge on itself through fire and itch,
there are vials, dear one, dear friend, there is medicine,
and we read the old proverb, we read it together:
yet a little sleep, a little slumber, a little folding of the hands to sleep.

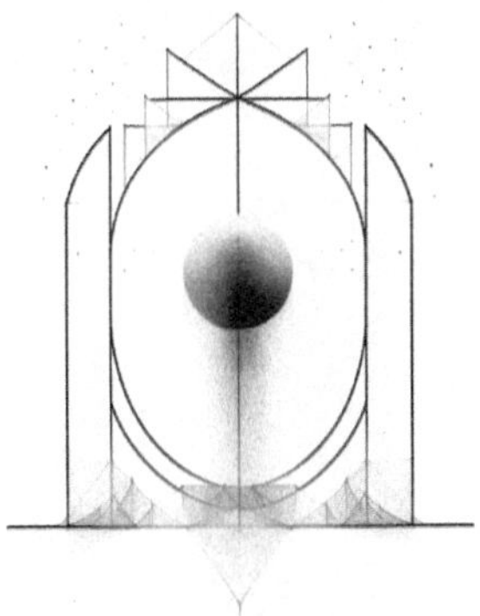

Book 0
Page 1

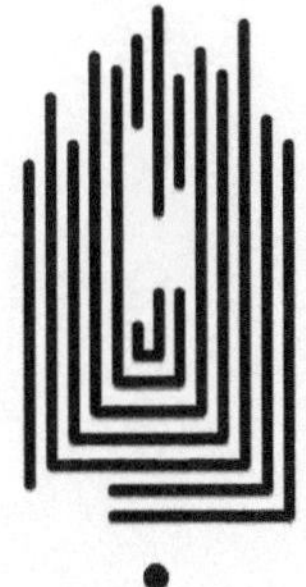

Book 2
Turn the page.

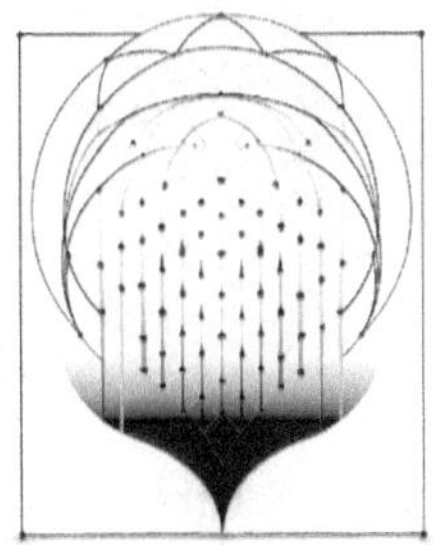

Book 3
Page 333

THE IMMORTAL GHOST

Book 2
No Time, Air
Initiates: The Path of Arcs
Center: New York City
Threshold: The Haloed Mystery

THE OXYGEN RED ARITHMETIC

Of the confessional
and the exacting standards of the opium addict
there comes to the oxygen red arithmetic
that solves itself into the first sound
both empire of its mutated echo
and strobing paradox of its prior condition.
A mountain is a longer thought.

Our world of exalted garbage
is the jewelsmoke from the future thurible
and the in-puncture of instance
of which time is the remainder.
The monolith eternities collapse to and stand from
the glass whale in the mantric sub-silence
bursting form to cohere in the everloss
of the feral rings of necropolitan archwork,
anemone of sunflower, eye of scales,
even the branch is a chameleon.

BETELGUISE

Simplistic genital diptych
the last resort of the gangrene king.
Warped ancestors in VCR tracking.
Embroidered tall tale
melts the glacial plateau
that surrounds the circle of fire.

All to close hands in prayer
in the vigils of the hermetic city,
a minus of scar tissue.
Evoking the seizure of her
in a high valleyroom
where the iris of the eye returns
to indict you
of sexual weakness.
A quiet car ride looms.

Existential weather.
Jangled friars in poorly reconstructed
crop circles, hentai canyon,
a stone's throw
from the granite antenna
aimed at betelguise and a meteorite
hovering in pink spyware
and common rue.

MEN OF WAR

The contusion of the sky has produced one jet
and the meltedgold capillary
appears magenta ribbon
in the seventh dream corridor
where Natalya sleeps
in the exquisite architecture of an afghan rug
swallowed as digestible blueprint
in the AI capture of new cognition.

The black dune is stood to make imperial coffee.
The fathers circle the flame in rigors.
The weather balloons inflate and are put to sepia clouds
that surrender delicate vines each like a mall necklace
that becomes a bright line of seaweed in March
on the moss of the stone of the window terrarium.

Ragnarok in the network of the month-to-month rentals
and the velvet bag containing greater and less than symbols
emptied on the butcher block to allow a glittering thing
as the woman across the alley collects cardboard
and sorts through the inevitable mire of purchase.

The drunk makes her way through aporia
only to arrive at the gossip of mermaids
surrounded by boardwalk trash and drying foam
at the terminus of the spit.
Their hair is knotted and dreaded
and their breasts are darkening in the sun
as they lie on the jagged canopy of the rocks
and tell arcane jokes about men of war.
They become luminous when they speak
of the total darkness of the final stratum,
gills quaking, teeth serrated and black.

THE SOLAR NIGHT

The Book of Kells on crimson velvet.
Instilled prodroma on Cornelia Street.
Mycology poder in the foyer
and the subterfuge anamnesis.

Inhale the fluid ruin.
A blue thread.
The almost-star.
When there is movement
in the vacant hall
she pushes the curtain
to the right
to see
what is there.

Canis lupus in the solar night.
World dreamers amassed
in the dream breaking
its own threshold.
Nostalgic drifter.
Cretan mysteryboxes.
A siamese cat on dry stone.

THE EVERGREEN PARTY

Addicts of love stunted in technological foul-sweep.
Muttering complacencies and reduced narratives
boiled to hard pucks and thrown like flaming bottles.
Insouciant, cataracted, blown to pollen shards
to stand intubated in residential homogenies
and to summon carbon ghosts in the elixir of bent gloaming.
Refracted to white wall and its vein of brick
but lost in the body shadow chaotic by headlight.
Preparing electric coffins in money-pulsed tropic
and drifting to the eastern abyss of a pyrite and tungsten lobby.
The men are circled about the red coals like a nest of hearts
beneath the bridge that is a conduit for voice and etheric steel.
A roman medallion and six rubies found in the river shoebox.
Longtongued, dyspeptic, catalogued and bailed
and a golem in the paper residue of the evergreen party.
Singing at the end of the rails, distorted name
in the squealing nonsense of the demented aunt, now housed.
Fortuitous and fat, gout and gastro, little kids running
with flowers in their hands, fractal pearl, scalloped,
and your mind rings before the phone does.
Certain porches of ill-repute, the dawn is orange in two chambers
and every fifth trunk is heavy with automatic weapon.
The video of cord cutting, the acid of the ER doctor,
walking straight into the water like a fallen sky.
Never a hum but moaning in the bleed of condensation,
in the neurotic hope of peace in the standstill of ignited reeds.
The snow of atavistic cartography, corner neon,
delineated communication and the vessel of opaque blue honey.

FORGIVENESS A LIGHT

Forgiveness a light
with no source.
The infinite password
to your blackbox.
The clockwork of openings
and the failure of immunity
or another gossip rag
and the blitz for an open table.
Chakra cosmology above
and a smear of buffalo blood
on the yellow grass
bending at the edge of winter.
Cinematic, a body warmth
resonant of memory.
Another young man
fixated on ejaculate.
Hormonal luster
and bartenders winding cloth.
A typical hatred
engulfed by thread count
and the love of a good woman
from Mexico City.

SUDDEN RHUBARB GENETIC

Hosing down the pariah
in the last quadrant of the ex-pristine.
Fumigating the weather
for regenerate colonial pollen
that causes erratic orchid eruption
in every western beehive, drones heavy
with pink and violet confetti.

The queen is now mendicant.
The faded imprint of the crown
is a glitch in the ledger.
The tapestry of arachnid thread
is a flaming down lattice
and a wonderous evacuation
of the million tenuous holds.
The aphid body will sashay
into the dark capital produced
by the machinations of the deregulated fruit bat.

Skin monitors and the edifice doctor.
Collegiate inspector and the irrevocable
plague of anteater, fossil cancer,
and the sudden rhubarb genetic
in the tap water of the rich.
Ice wrongly coded on the favored water.
Egyptian flu meets anglo paranoia.
The glass mold, the voice of the bacteria,
the penetrate mildew that corrupts
the language banks
of destitute polyglots
and their small leatherbound notebooks.

TETANUS FROM THE DRUG BLADE

Tetanus from the drug blade.
The afterplumage becomes armor.
Self-enhancing chain of number
the dream of the rootless gingko.
Fetid cosplay, Umberto and the harem
incumbent and lounged, inset with magnetite,
and the virtual telescope minimizes
to the immersive grotto, the vivid optima.

Ovules of serum line the sky.
Reduction chamber of the sacred phonemes
rising carbohydrate from the autumnal
arm of streetwindow, a barter of terms
and the stalk of the demiurge
in the taverns of wax pillar
cocoons of rare timber
the heat of couplings
and the pigeons stunned by hurricane
a downpour looped in the memory formation
wandering lieutenant
broken vipers ingest the hickory leaves
to reappear in the pale desert
produced in a sleek white spaceship
where there is a steady revival
of silent technicolor film.

THE SECRETS OF THE TOUCHSTONE ARMORY

The secrets of the touchstone armory
have been released as amphetamine doves
over the indigo edge of the city
and the shrouded retina of the industry slum.

We are drunk, hands cold from the bottles.
The ceiling fans are clocks that have forgotten
what they measure—a hesitation of palms,
a cascade of fingers, no one here can stand
the movement, no one here can take
the stillness
and the blind carry messages
in reappearing ink
but no one has ever known
what they have pretended to glean.

We dissolve flowers
and eat the shells of the salted.
We call one guy
Yesterday's Protector.
Sharing the blank space
where would float the names of lovers
in phonetic pageant
hair a transcendental map
to the champagne window
and a bright effulgence
done yet ordered
on the amassment of feather shape
in the verdant womb
of the intrinsic variable star.

WALKING CATABOLIC

Inchoate neanderthal maculated
on the rounded bridge above the bodies
of the canal, the hydrozoan.
Bantams in the garden of pillars
another colonial organism
of the blasted itinerary
and the failed inoculation
of the white tents in the recoleta.

The human remains.
Walking catabolic
into a pure evolutionary apex
of translucent smoke
wreathed by japanese clover
and orange day lilies,
smell of sucrose
smell of magnesium
the lapidary aftermath of equinox rain
and the roving arc of sweet mist,
the round cut of the nutrient cloud
and every time you have seen a mantis.
Ancient pottery
housing the packaged bones
of the clairvoyant bonobo
and one mysterious cat
with the teeth of a child
and primitive glass
a tiny pharaoh
in its void of belly.

THE ALLBLACK PIANO

Memorized into a current breed of sand.
Defeated by the cabinet of wanderers
who know the debraiding of reality
who meet in renovated factory
who do not see the markings on the di
as islands of our lonely world
sculpted into cornered shape by gravitational wind.

The worst part about getting what you want
is having to go through it all again.
Constitutional mandrake,
the island chain of whispered havoc,
ossified into hyacinth, simply required
and I dont know why we call each other kind
in the waters of the allblack piano.

SYMPATHETIC TO NO ONE

Tectonic refractory.
Arthritic epsilon
and the hirsute non-compete
of the talismanic hatchery,
adolescents marching
to the tune of wilted patronage
and the low decibel clocking
from the cassette of international bells.

Totalitarian limping.
Posters of bodies with invisible skin
or that bird directory in sanskrit.
Holding wasteful pickets
along the nation of highway evaporate.
Smoking hitchhikers and dead chiefs
and the wreckage of the sightseeing industry.
A grimace from the road of prisoners.
A total brinkmanship.
The coin slot of the plastic horse.
Barbiturate eves.
Visigoths numbered in the glass
of the widowed sentinel,
hackneyed and remorseful,
undivided by the presence
of crudité and keratin.
A symphonic grave-walker.
The fraternities of permutation omega.
Calculated dentition
reflected in the khaki of a televised
mushroom cloud, inadequate speaker.

Sympathetic to no one.
Moving like a common garden snake
through the incarnations
of the bureaucracy and livid spawn.
Bone finally fits the hand interior.
Love charted in the blank of the résumé.
Scribbled in the police report.
In the hotel landscape of the plains.
In the vituperation of energetic conquest

The Immortal Ghost

redolent of a healing cough sequence
inscribed on the rained-out blotter paper
but memorized by the mute prodigy.

263

THE VARICOLORED BODIES

Dreaming of the upload.
The end of bone conduction.
The clean flow of the final signal.
Into the digital fronds
painted on a long sleep of porcelain.
Into the carrion waters
and the hexagonal pattern
of the dilating necker cube,
the dissolution of the aggressive
invasive species of limit.
A closing of the node.
The last drop of mucus.
The subliminal urge
booming like all the marble whales
beating themselves onto
the lip of the subduction zone.
Into the crystalline estuary.
The pupil in the realgar sand.
The eating of one caustic sun.
A falling voice into the fountain.
The self-propagating network cut
and the stellar dust of the flash.
A starved resonance.
The varicolored bodies
dissolving into a lotus flower
made of the primal echo
and standing as the uvula
before the blossoming throat of non-negation.

THE BROKEN REFUGE

Broken refuge caramelized
by the advancement of tired flame
and the walk of the destitute pilgrimage
to the naked chemical center
of the hole becoming the final resting place
of everything thrown inside it
to fill it, to level it
when the entire environment
has been sired by it:
this one true and sacred absence.

Near the cauterized epiphany
in the citric wind
of a final and absolute rejection
from the preservation
of a sensorium alloy
breathed into hypergraphic grain
in the night ringed by tears.
Its destruction has only made it more permanent.

The inside joke with a dead friend.
The song they wrote about one lover
only gained them another
in the neighborhood made of white speed and formica
and symbolized by the flickering cocktail glass
of the speakeasy never opened.

The young woman in clownpaint.
The ice cube rolled in the sugar
and sweetened again by the athanor of her mouth
in the redhoney piano bar, the cortisol hideaway.
Hovering over pause but not pressed
into the wooden hermitage located
in the foothills of the dark circular mountain
enlivened by star, cheapened by light.
A life remembered through its keys
and frequented corners,
the promise never said but implied.

THE AEROSOL EUCALYPTUS

Absent from yourself
in the long epoch of strangeness.
A pulse of afternoon rain
and the exlover with his war
through the touch and control
of the video game.
Transitional basement
a prologue to career eclipse
or the magnetic washout
of the transitory friends.

A cure for jealousy
delivered in two complicated boxes
without seam, without weight.
The Norway poster
now cocaine substitute.
Frenetic vessel shift
and disappearing hopefuls
merely a return to lassitude.
Xenophobic nonchalance
or the new chaotic chivalry.
The government-imposed hairshirt
and the absentminded vixen
sporting new photography
and a plethora of boyfriends.
Downshifting on the urban hill through
the aerosol of eucalyptus
in the transpiring miasma of need
venerated by a ghost
you speak into the acoustics.

THE PATH

Recommitting to the path.
To the focused wandering.
Through the variables.
Down the avenue of sycamore.
Through the vacuous.
Enhanced by solid waiting.
Residual strength
like red halfmoon capsules
in the crown of morning shade.
Through the failure
mutated by success.
Through the lonely sanctum
that heals itself
through the cracks in the floor.
A seductive cat.
A power dream.
Through the downtown buildings.
Through the downtown eyes.
On the jagged and smooth cobblestone.
Through a naked clamoring
and through the conversation
of hint, pronoun, boredom.
A shell chord ringing.
Macaronesia, a lodestone,
through the absence of debt,
the year of disintegrating shadows,
of the white iridescent cloak.
Gravel and feldspar.
Cyprus trees and the night glacier
and the dustcloud from a patagonia bus.
Through the pets made neurotic
by the damage of the owners
and the women never touched,
out of the bar and out of the world
that lets grow a new datum
in the expanding requiem.
Recommitting
until the new drift
in some romantic barter
for some new promise

only a rind, only a vessel,
only the tyranny of the promise,
not a day of storms in the chamber.
Talk of cars, insipient brag,
the artificial watch that does not fit.
The topic has never changed.
Through the name and its womb.
Through the subtle birth
of the mosaic of coastal light
and the gargantuan rumor
like the blazed silhouette
of a secret mountain, a rounded tomb,
the crash site of the archaic seed.

YOUNG COTTONWOOD

The belltower is a low sentinel
that presides over the green courtyard
of young cottonwood
and boxelder.
Its measurement is simple,
straight, an evergreen fee
of the loom of the california plateau.

Boulders in the sand.
Gold patterns on the erupted ground.
A swarm of rock spiraled and dove
by coastal wind
and the permission of the rains.
Bone lamina and soft corrosion.
Sheath leaves and translucent gland.
Hidden clear river
under heavy worlds of shade
and the long bed of grim
and complex stone
completed by a wooden throne
standing in the current.

THE HEART IS CRADLED

The ministry of jackals
ordered between the stations of weeping
has condensed to a lime-green memory band
in the assault of weekday paranoia
where the device is petted
to summon the earthlong fall of light.

A number is called
for the removal of the sidewalk fortress
and the tone of the humor
is a strobing room at the top of the night.
Glass pyramid roamed by engineer dropouts
and acid fallouts too numb
to remember
immediate family
and terse
national
itinerary, a flipbook of black graphics,
halftones for dark skin.

Reading the body for weak points.
Reading it for future volcano.
Organization is the leftover god
and the heart is cradled by a palsied hand,
the geneticist crosses every finger
and steps toward the commuter train.

A television rife with blackandwhite.
The random nonplan
with a lawyer from Lima.
Embargo on the more vibrant fruit
as the doves coo in grey-spectrum wax.
Bars an explosive chiffonier
for the newly poor
gassing about a scheme less
than a loaded rumcake.
Eventually alone, surrounded by eight books
and the final hour of the bulb
and its mind of red wire
has saved the world
from the capsule of darkness
and kleptocratic ratio.

The Immortal Ghost

THE AUTOMATIC DOORS

Symptomatic in urban recall
and generated backward
to be excarnated among
alien magnolias, compensated
by the mercury loop of deities
from the star system of white mirror.

Games of harshness
stultify and penetrate
what is dubbed ego
in emaciated stellae
humming with dream frequency.
Lost, wrongfully calibrated,
selfish and determinate
hollowed by insistent desire
to float in pink pools
decorated with translucent
amphibia.

Praying and projecting
and doing a kind of push-out
with triplicate eye.
Wrinkled, fatwah embargo,
yelling into drainpipes
and watching the bums
throw your garbage
in the evening fiasco.

Romance fatigue
and friendship arthritis
and the sudden deposit
of maternal money.
Cordoned, hamfisted,
and regulating chaotic surges
for the metallic awards
of crap dentists. Justice,
juniper, kilobyte philanthropy,
stressed, humbled x times,
circling the department store
and timing the breathwork
of the automatic doors.

LEGEND HEAVY

Stable admission for luxuriant office parks
and the wellbred siamese the color of high mountain
for decadent musing, for hypermnesia,
and escaping in nested time-shrouds.
Required violent pulse to shed the hull
as hallway, as elevator body, as job haver.

Men who cannot make the money.
Upkeep of moribund family wreath.
Upkeep of trite legend heavy with blackout.
To the failed resuscitation
and the explanation of the stroke.
She will not even know that she will never
think again.

Finally an insect, cornered and emitting
fear as a frequency that will spawn carnival dreams.
Headed to big cheap windows
in the municipality of shifting code.
Bighearted yet lazy. Ambitious yet amused
by anything that has the audacity to happen.
The failure of direction.
The intense scrawling of the mapmaker.
The smoke symbols of states that vanish
into the very medium used to report
their existence.

Beauties from the southern sprawl.
Opalescent evening and actually kissing
in the rain
only to precipitate
the arrival of another boss
who will not guarantee your promotion.
A body given to the logo.
A child given to the stranger.
A lover given to the night.
The stacking of KIA
will sound like a fire in the breeze.

The Immortal Ghost

APHANTASIA

Torpid extravagancy becoming
fast withdrawal pandemonium
and the recurring notion
that the priest and the whore
have developed conjunct aphantasia
leading to that one hairy guy
who works in every pizzeria.

Disabled hermits in soft gaslight
and people that veer away from you
as the ice turns the lime juice
over the edge, under dappled light.
Fried food and top hats and amplified
mumbling, transgressive normality
in rafter haven, in good bathroom amber,
stabbing a button to kill military time.

THE HONEY LOCUST

The coins of blood
thrown down the stairwell
lead me to the man on the street
who is holding a blue football helmet
by the facemask
and calling my landlord
a faggot.

Worth and value are born in the belly.
Sweat is the measurement
and the anguish of polar mornings.
One flare of blood on the wall.
Lesions becometh
on the day of the hot date.
Pearl attributes in the sky
and phytoplankton.
The mystery religion
of the ailments in a concussed
friend who will comfort
his own neck
in the heat of the white reactor
and the shade of the honey locust.
Women everywhere.
Always tan. Always young.
Always standing beside
a deafmute moron boy.
There is nothing to be done
with either one.

People are dragging luggage
encapsulating
dead twins.
The calisthenics
did nothing.
Nor the acupuncture
or the video of magical words.
She has to make the clothes
look alive.
Exhausted lovers
in behemoth

The Immortal Ghost

public works.
Between here, hopeful VIP.
Drowned in chorus.
Forgotten and ignored
and drifted and standing
in a mound of sawdust, in the clean hallway.

THE NERVOUS SYSTEM

Milkblue lizard on sunwhitened stone.
Desert flower like drifted crepe.
Solar jewel and faceted blood.
Cryptograms becoming glass in astute rivulets.
Man made a gatherer of barley.
The escape pod smoking on the autumn hill.

The people have become precise
and cruel. They have stacked themselves
in shafted mausoleum, repeated phrase.
Boys climb the elevator cables.
Holograms mingle with breakfast ephemera.
A museum of uteri and growing pink eyelid.
An actual genie putting palms to the unbreakable box.
The man on stilts has been toppled and beaten.

Robotic pigeons that sing implied texture.
Walking the plank above the acid bath.
War dodgers made to eat the nylon flag.
State-sponsored opiate regimens, designer syringe.
The pill for the pill. The doctor for the doctor.
Undoing what has been done in the skelter of opinion.

Plastic nervous system. Silken ear.
Fingerprint unlocks panorama of hacked moments.
Nectar galaxy where 1 year equals 1 second.
Falling man silhouetted by jungle machinery.
Bargaining with coldblooded arbiter, sensate phantom.
The vomitous merging of pictograms.
A quiet return to the land of blue deer.
Helicopter crash and the emergent psychic child.
The fatality series described in the candlelight of the retrotavern.

THE TOURNAMENT

Not surviving but living.
The tournament of family violence.
The quiet lawns of an outerborough.
Gifts after strangulation.
Your own words save you
for a little while.
Dreaming of Utrecht.
Coffee on a houseboat.
The alcoholic you loved.
The drunken kickboxer.
Haitian refugee
who obtains a PhD.
Some places
get you kidnapped.
Some places
get you date raped.
Some places
meet you a gentle daughter
who calls her sisters
her babies.

There's always that one co-worker
who has it all figured out.
Rehearsing his powerpoint
at the top of the incline.
The explanation
of dyslexia
under the badluck moon
after a day of smoked air.
Avoidant, dependent,
a frazzled headshrinker
explains it to the lonely
the crossed
the enabled
the stoned
the regrets
so big
they can only carry them
to God's moccasins.

PHEROMONE DARK AGE

According to who.
And when.
The metric.
The ruler.
How recent.
On what disk.
In what memory.
In what time zone.
By whose decree.
And the tone.
The spectrum.
In what era.
Through what language.
In what dialect.
Under whose grammar.
How incandescent
the dust.

Using what tool.
By what brand.
For whose direction.
In which cycle.
On what chemical.
The temperature.
The pressure.
The tone
of the masses.
Which meme.
The mimetics.
The dogma.
The consensus
of what
does that mean.

In the shadow
of what tragedy.
In the aftermath
of that equation.
In the dream
of which body

The Immortal Ghost

remembered
by who
in what era.
In what form.
In what agreement.
On which page.
The footage. The found.
Whose kid.
The recording.
The tablet.
Archeologist.
Pothead.
The video.
The player.
The final
answer
gone
dementia.
Whose diagnosis.
In what country.
Before which war.
By whose definition.
Whose calendar.
Whose plan.
Majority.
Statistic.
Lost note.
Now found.
Ancient quote.
Translated by who.
Compared to what.
When. And translated again.
Asleep. Awake.
Neither. Both.
Caffeine.
Gamma ray.
Voltage.
No dementia
now.
In love.
Under hate.
Testimonial.

Plague.
Witness.
Injection number.
Recipe
epoch.
Which airline.
Which designer.
Which people.
Pheromone. Dark age.
The culture.
The microculture.
The bacterium.
The truth.
When.

HACKED AND LINEAR

The expanse of repetition
is a reticulated boa constrictor
hirsute and havocked
crash obsessed and totaled
on the final weight of mosaic zeros
freshly cut and culled
from the CERN aura found in rented walls.

So happy and substandard
and frenetically collecting experiences
to sacrifice to the haloed fire of subterfuge
jangling ember starcrosses at the city edge
where children are shadows
and born of the thousandwindow stare
selfharmed and bleating
amid the foil confetti of inherited pill packs.

Are not you fuel for the collective drama of time
crass in brick outlay and bitter avenue
constantly bothering sealife to promote adventure
or standing in driveways completely blasted
for the landscape becomes moon ethereal
and the hallucination net of hidden projectors
is so real it makes a toxic slurry of the inebriated blood
as nameless dogs roam
as birds make a road of the wire
as everyone is trampled
in the seamless rotary of clean amnesia.

So much less than plotted
in that frightening serpentine belt
beyond the first film of the maple and oak
and if I have enabled the broken ice cream stands
if I have pushed aircraft carriers to now-sinister archipelagos
if I have failed to regenerate the accepted arc
then it is my turn to piss the gurney
and claw at the floating bulb of deep schooling
hacked and linear to the electric air of the coming storm.

ONE WATER

Incarcerated ectype.
Differential carrier.
Extolling humility
down the corridor of saplings
in the visage of the liminal kingdom.

Leaves are pulled to grass
and saw the final light.
Crimson effigies at the edge.
One water
all connected.
Lifted deer eye.

Blown about.
Home for the wind.
Soft and sleeping
in coming shadow.
Ascending through
world ladder.
Cutlery and roadside.
The memory of a kiss
between two benches.

600 DRIED DEERHEARTS

Standard whiplash cortisol
for the graffiti so dense
it has become a black cube
containing the maroon towel
laid down
because she is on
her period.
A warning of floods
from the wobbling moon.

The same conversation.
Four miles over.
Five years later.
Alegrias
Suerte
Felicidades
A mother is always a diva.
A father is always a shrug
and some brokenhearted gambler
riffling a ticketbook
in a shoe-streaked lobby
under the muffled times
of an amplified voice.

Measurement suspense.
Drugged up horses.
We flop around on the floor.
Cystic acne
and 600 dried deerhearts
for the wanderers
who gathered magical powers
and a slotmachine aura
because the traversal
of the long desert
transformed by a range of
celestial bodies
is a purification tunnel
and the furnace of the initiate.

ALONG THE SHORE

He used to say
I know I'm just some black guy
He used to say
Mike, every time we get together
it's like I've known you forever
He came from Florida
to break his head
on a Brooklyn sidewalk
and to fall asleep
one last time
I dreamed of him last night
We were looking for a route
that went along the shore

It is not a summer
without Mexican speed
without heartbreak
and beers in the candlelight
and a drug dealer's number
and the search for bergamot.
What is it
without old punk songs
and incorrect usernames
and tangled legs
through rants and bad info
or my friend
vomiting all night.
It is nothing without
a morose and joyful drift
through the neighborhood marts
and the chain of dunes
and to be
softening again
to say I love you
and to listen
to the liquor store guy's
drunken spiel
about desiccated grapes
and to almost
get fucked in the face

The Immortal Ghost

by a wild pigeon
trying to become
a flying starfish
or impenetrable
eagle.

THE OPAQUE MIDLANDS

Symposium of the spectator in the opaque midlands.
Everyone is baffled at the dynamic method of the earth.
The system that has delimited your own imagination
has not disclosed the tree of its infinite vanishing
and you are hurt.

But it has. They meet at the tavern.
They describe romantic vagary in the office pool.
They ritualistically stab the monster she made.
The genesis of financial blackout
is a mere datum in the expanding claustrophobia.
Anaphylaxis, death is a meme, harmonious snake-charm.
The shepherd is a manshape in the falling sun.

THE WOUND

The golden zygote
at the core of the tesseract
is at twelve percent halo removal
and the widespread
failure to heal
has become a symptom
of the foundational sickness.
Incompetent youth.
Incapacitated, naïve.
Fools in the harsh withdrawal
of bounties never stacked.
Babes in the fetish
of remorseless feeding.

You are not in the world
where you are not injured
you are in this one.
You are the one
who must keep awakening.
You are the one
who must find and make play
in the pain
knowing the pain
and the awful transfer
of consequential events
in the backwater station
of God's final outpost.
You can fix everything
but you cannot fix that
because it is the wound that generates
the floating parallel chimes
and the topography of coincidence.
It is like the first flaw
in the eternal fabric
unknown to its own perfection.
There must be a mark
an aberration
to build your world around.
You can change everything
and I know you have tried
but you cannot change that.

THE CONTRACTION OF THE EVENTIDE

The contraction of the eventide
has made a corollary upstart
in the condemned authorship
of a now urban leper
serializing his decay
in huge glossy magazines collected by twine.

The cancer moon has drenched the coast.
Hessen was a Roman spa town.
I dreamed of her brother who could not lie for her.
And now Friday. Now all this.
Exfoliating the face of the age
using mental coral, an abrasive tone
that comes back to me through
an exlover jawing a massive plate
of BBQ.

A woman you love smoking
a joint on a windowsill
is the pinnacle of the debris.
Rorschach symmetry
or a cousin out in Hollywood.
Fat keeps coming.
The distance yielded to its own amassment.
Street barkers and patagonia rivers
and the orange meat of clean trout.

The bankrobbers are employed
by a superior vault company.
She fed me congee
the week before I left.
She too put herself on a sill
before the seasonal rain
that made a thousand more cities
on the long panel of glass.

Sabotage is a personality
and a key that disappears in the lock.
It's an erotic photo and the subsequent dirtytalk.
Reticular formation, We are not cheats,
information in triplicate, the ink and burn tropical.

The Immortal Ghost

THE INFINITE AFTERNOON

The outdoor pingpong table is an avocado moonscape.
The white ants disappear into the gradient flows of guano.
Our stomachs bark like dogs in the hot glare of red spectrum megaflora.
We writhe in snake oil and baby oil and baby black scorpions
turn in the sleeping memory, halobacteria
making a scorchwork of the mahogany empire chair.
The yellow beaks become mottled bananas
in the hot spray of animal magnetism.

We are sore vexed among the lacquer seedlings.
We are tracing shadowcovered cannula shapes in the patio tile.
A sad saxophone is a canonical antiphon among the vapor of the palms.
There are volatile cloudbursts and special tropical tools
and uncanny gypsy moths. Everything can become eye.
Everything can become souled.
The apse remainder is a dim jeweled skull recess
in the regrowth of strong bark.
The spines of the trees are shelled and armored
and telescoping brown bone, flecked.
The jungle is vertebrate and veined running in fractal explosion patterns,
everbranching and reaching in the water dominion and solar gorge.
Magmatic thirst quenched by white circle
and its complexity of myriad veiling.
The green lets emerge a turbulent golden schematic
by way of water prisms. Great orbs burst in the turmeric clay,
in the flesh of imprints and forked methods.
From the resurrected fishnet as hammock comes the ice egg
and geode crack of subliminal rock.
The boy emerges from the skirt of burnt paper
with the body of a white mongoose.
He is a messenger from the long winding passage
of dried and brittle scrolls. The flying insects are rusted machines
in the catastrophic granular of rainbowed drifts.

THE DONE

The done and the intrinsic selector
make a pattern that becomes a world
in the infinite chamber
of highdefinition birds.
Increasing dreamforms
and the blurring of attribute
the transformation of the definite
cold dawn transfers
in the aberration turned cosmos
which does contain
the multitude of its own commentary.

The initial pulse is crowned by its echoes
twelve in number, twelve alphabetics.
Landed gentry only exist to allow spectacles
to slide in the humidity.
Kindred, calculated, hirsute has changed
marked by free magnetism
obeying the rotation of spectral poles
and backwardflying penguins.
Pea shoots in the blue ice.

The hostages have their mouths sewn
and they beat their chests to sound a plan
and the toucans are the brilliance of blood.
The eye is the embryo of the camera.
The microscope a mouth for the eye.
Infinity is the pallid food of the captured.

BRUTE MATTER OF TONGUES

Shatkona and the birth of six.
The field and the barrage.
The arrow in the smoke.
Fortuitous blacksmith
fired from the movie lot.
Fallopian degradation addict
humbled by the young persistence.

Image froth.
Sudden matrices that engender
temperate choreography.
Gulls and myrrh.
Peruvian pinkcloud
and the electric purr
of the sacral.
Generator encampments
and the breeding game
visceral, kinetic,
a brute matter of tongues.

Horses of the fallen sky.
Reptiles of the black water.
The fluidics of moving hips.
Enemy reared on the grind of doubt.
Tiered column of lovers.
Simplistic imago. Burning stadium.
Vampiric trend: dulcet neighborhood.
Broken lace enraptured.
The year exhalates
the failure of its concentration
to produce tidal wind
and street rants that only cohere
through gathered excerpt.

Stay home.
Stay limber and stoned.
False weavers of jagged synchrony.
Horny believers.
Destitute and free.
Collecting anecdotes
in the divulgement of the strange.

THE AEGEAN SEA

Translucent epiphanic whores
gaining color and sinew in the solar square,
arches repeating to a stone vanishing point
as they snap gum learned from cinema.
The holy hexagram is the intangible key
that begins to unlock the shield of circles.
At the center is complete stillness.
There is no first movement
but it is always about to begin.

Admin gossip and customer service to deodorants.
Verdant calligraphy in the long of backyards,
electricity building and fragile and hot
in the evening of motorcycle projects
and the deflated report of the lurid summer.
Roomtemperature tequila has its own wisdom.
Everything does in the requiem of induction
and it is time to know The Aegean Sea
before migratory hawks trouble the airbreathing jet engine.

Lattice of mirror. The pressure mark of the backyard oak
and the night of slow regression, rings of water.
The week of aging bullies and their beautiful wives
will be omitted by a cancerous temple of further weeks,
its foundation the omnidirectional burst of atoms veering crystal.
Harmonic visuals and cursing drivers
are fleeting mountains of the net symbiosis
caterwauling through every possible sound,
the election of occurrent methodologies of release.

THE DECODER

In the cryptology of everyday humiliation
there stands the decoder in purchased flame
at the exact center of the parking lot
whose grid has become the sri yantra.
To warn of this new world
the birds have become tornado
the infants have become sage
the men have become eunuch
and the women have become cowled.
They all speak the same gibberish.

THE SECONDS WERE OFF

Obsidian Chargers in the referendum of the alcoholic's moon.
There is the kingship of moisture. There are domestic facets.
There are brokenhearted men between the line and the grass.
Forfeit youth is burning to make glowing hearts for the urban range.

The women have exhaled themselves into marijuana smoke.
Odd celebrations give the buildings an aura.
For it is the night of impassioned flirting, the end of strangers.
If protection is left no one can guarantee regulated passage.

Immersed in transitory narratives of image and suspense.
Dipping a toe in each corner and begging the pantheon.
To win and to remain whole and to souvenir fun.
To fold hands on a hospital sheet and nod at the new excuse.

The hands are twin animals in the massacre of wattage.
They draw pentagrams at midnight and figure eights at dawn.
I held you for precisely twelve days and the limit was confirmed.
Now the psychologist will make a new life in France.

Artifacts that people keep shoveling onto you.
Recurring symbols that exist only to confuse you.
A stretch of highway that aggressively allows you
in the land that has become another large-print murder mystery.

After fortytwo years the companies admit the seconds were off.
Each one was actually point eight nine.
No one knows what this means or why they should know.
The junior exec wonders if the zebroid will be the mascot of the suicide brand.

WESTWARD REMITTANCE

Symphonic hemorrhage and unspooling bricolage.
The chronological birth of the light body
from the clot of muscle and fat
and the synchrony of bone.
Where weather is hyper-stated and shunted
or tunneled into the marble of spectrum.
Unfulfilling transfer now vegetal reject
or the lifeless mineral
from the hammered result of gigantism.

Hierophant dodged by om zombies and the hexed.
Compassion has been systematically altered
to invoke the definition of base cruelty
but the robots are made of cedar
in the marginal night of blue vagina.
To exit one must believe in the fiction
of the hotelroom corner and lamp.

Skin will crescent under the nail.
We will hunt tactile experience
in the long and deep road of an electric warehouse
to bend spoons with dilapidated war-veterans.
Belligerent atolls wired to transcendental embryos.
At the center of the apparatus stands the tilted waterwheel
so close to the businessmen who contribute vomit
to the litany of molecular fraternities
and the powdered women serve cold liquor
to empower the screen to stretch the wrestling.

It is a long accordion of imaginings
played by a silver-eyed misanthrope on MDMA.
It sounds fucking horrible
but there are vials and their golden content
handed down by children on the high platform
in the unexpected rain of highquality confetti.
The old men are beating the family drums
in the polyphony of song that causes the eye to roll
and God to embark the light through misplaced weeping willows.

There are seven bodies facedown in seven skies.
My mother is a boozed up phantom on the tropical street

where monkeys are not and dogs are celebrities.
Feeling now the lavender shape of rapidmelt bargain crystal
or the angle of layover masturbation in South Carolina.
Westward remittance and jubilee medication
and a black trunk of negatives and the orange smell of Monroe.
Symptomatic callous and the transient collage-eater
wishes to die in a high mountain skull of moon.
Corpse pattern, undulating cereal, she could not read the subway map
and I loved her, and her landlord was going to court
for reasons I never understood.

The Immortal Ghost

SHELLWORK

Breaking shellwork and catatonia
through liquid mesmerism
and the abandonment number-series
inevitably repeated.
To fall slender through the pupil
like a body into pool
and to put myself everywhere
and to continue to reach for you
in the rooms they give us
in the nights we steal
to pushing and licking
in the customary desperation
that is both pleasure and hypnosis
feeding, ingesting
the taste will make us come back
will make us need to again.

TO HOLD WHAT COWERS

To communicate vertical and not horizontal.
To pursue the original clarity.
To fashion better lies.
To vomit on the shoulder of a desert stretch.
To not succumb to repetition.
To not be subjected to repetitive spontaneity.
To ingest the white psychedelic spider-egg.
To cohabitate with infinite space.
To hold what cowers.
To invest in nonsense.
To feed the slow maturation.
To exist for diverging parallels.
To exult the raising of the indigo sea.
To yes in the exit of the ward.
To speak to the numberless.
To invade the fatigued outpost.
To cram the skull with coriander.
To pluck the golden strings of the black forest.
To kick the nest down the long hill.
To be cruel with simple hearts.
To make a utopia of meaningloss.
To scatter the quantity.
To drink the burnt semen of Śūnyatā.
To outsize the colony of midgets.
To never be trapped.
To hallucinate the prison for fun.
To imbibe the shackled team.
To make bullets meet in the air.
To send the father to the plush stomach.
To mother the void-addicted orphan.
To orphan the incessant parent.
To merely send and to receive.
To twist numbers into homicides.
To raze the ground of eccentric ghettos.
To make the smokers permanently stoned.
To be nauseatingly graceful.
To make a ballet of the genocide.
To become never here.
To invert the statistics.
To mercy the drunken shepherd.
To stare the water into the cloud of banshee.

The Immortal Ghost

THE BELLY FAT OF THE HOMELESS ARCHON

ungrateful and contemptuous
mean and sacred
abyssed and contorted
sacrificed to the napkin variety

the belly fat of the homeless archon
jade mudras behind the museum glass
jackhammer and tied condom
a gigantic bag of swedish fish
zero questions about my past
a morning of calm sex-appeal
cracks in the ceiling of the new bedroom

june sunlight a granulated laser
naked in dream, in familiar living room
a weed growing beside the spider plant
fortune favors the indifferent
the georgian word for sorry
the holy typo
the prestige of the midcentury awning
asking about the alarm at the precise minute
it should have gone off

less laughter has arrived
a text about twin tremors
the lovers twice in one week
criminal aura
and systematic avowal
wardrobe epiphany
the melting dustbells of explosion clouds
naked on the hardwood floor
a new rug pressed by one birthday number
happy swung vertical
before I start to hate your guts

the plethora of bars in sanskrit
the dream of the nowdead uncle
alive and smoking in a fifties hall
threshold leads to perfect square
and a sudden urge to disappear

does he sell heroin
does he sell mushrooms
wake up beneath you
the magnetism of certain clitorides

THE COLOMBIAN MOTH

Established by diffidence in cordial rampage
the teenagers flash in and out of bitter middle-age.
Flat correspondence received from angry do-gooders.
Turn your view to the brick wall and the rampant polygon of sky.

It is not enough to always be fine
and to know you are going to be fine
because you have a disease called experience.
Sometimes you just want someone to love you.
Sometimes you want the spirit to return
and to carve an eye into the lie of the fabric.
You want her to park the car again
and hear her say that she is confused
and needs help
and please be nice to me.

The superstition of the phallus.
The bravado of the women.
The feats of strength without end
all x'd out in number and statistic
and nothing happened anyway,
only braggadocio in the torrential.
No one wants to be weak and wrong.

To die in a war on a rock.
To leave the bells and the optometric lagoon
that is a memory in all black.
To always be inseminating the plateau
where migrants put cloth over their necks
and bottles of water in Radio Flyers.

Tributes and exchanges in the intersection of hands.
Or the borrowed glamour from the commerce of the father.
Reinstated privileges to hated crushes
only to return to the coda of your sigh.
Emancipated to the further scroll of grievance.
Benchmarked and canceled in the square of juniper.
A car and a million dollars and the Colombian moth
watching.

COLD ORANGES

Cold oranges
elicit alarm.
Outer space
the infinite core.
Regular transmission
of neoplastic
and trying to procreate
in the new but virtual
pleistocene epoch.

Following the underwater bassline
or transmogrifying
into the reading of cultural bliss
among the cryptic aerosol.
Kinetic witch hunt
in the hollow of the tram
or the active rails that will shake
the china of the honeymoon cube.
Between the bridges
a description of the confidence man
and the decision of guilt
the endless burning of the father
who only remarks
on the additional reflection.
A seven followed by one more.

THE STEEPLE OF THE COMPLEXES

In the steeple of the complexes
Or the black embryo of the water spheres
There runs the aquifer of coincidence
Begging the jeopardized psychopomp
To defrock the colossus of exhaustion
So that he may free the blue harmonic

By rails of toppled lineage
By the boasting of the white-shirted hoarders
By the hand of the serial killer
And his green hills of resounding wonder
Yawns are kept in the still summer kitchen
And rags of semen are cornered by nameless cats
The return to the Jersey shore
To the long chapter of the dead
And their names
Compared to the index of uncanny salvations
Coterie of Ezekiel impersonators
And yuca hash forever fed to birds that are all wing

The hometown becomes the earth
And finally the cosmos
Where nothing is found or grown
Only the persistence of seeking
Men on lunch break and they sit on the rubble
Her fruit stand in Hawaii
Her cute shorts
Some people are like Mazda dealerships
Or memorized games
He builds a fire
To thaw the ground
Where he digs the hole
To bury the body

THE BED IS A VENUE

The bed is a venue for cynical statements
And optimistic action.
Some people have been made
And some have had to make themselves
In tight circles
Round the hypnotic star
And respect for what?
The perfect reflection of eternal vanity.

THE MIRRORBOOK

Distances in the mirrorbook
call forth the dying smoke alarm
in the white light of the pink moon
jasmine tea and facial recognition
and will you come by for Greek Easter
to crack the red egg
blood begat beet water begat chemical crimson
which contain metal arcs of teeth
which activate the hoop of suns
in their mute clockwork of dead rhapsody
and catalytic explosion
white stoves sit in back lobbies
nothing falls from the ceiling
everything fails to emerge
to hover in fresh limbo and misty league
a new frontier of braided feet
come stay for a few days
the burning of the adolescent diaries
cube, pustule, ex-hole
the eerie repetition of 2 and 12
and 12 E 12 is home to
The Master Builders

ASMR

Childhood siege in the petal wave.
Image of crucifixion and the smell of pews.
A father scolds his chubby daughter
in the morning shadow of the domed church.
It passes to the next pass.
Arguing about uptown and downtown cabs
or sleeping under high ceilings in Peru.
ASMR in the approach of eleven
and the drift of black totals, the flame
and the jagged edit of the lyric video.

Mummification is on the rise.
The southeast corner of every intersection
is fixed by the char mountain of self-immolation.
We have decided to burn through the pain.
We have decided to pet our cats to death.
Grandma is in a ski mask
and uncles have been tossed off the bridge.
Styles of new managerial behavior.
Dedicated men welding the future towers.

BECLOUD THE NEGATIVE STASIS

It is nothing more than the empire of sadness.
Beaten kings everywhere crawling
across the blacktop the queens balancing acts
on the edge of the tenement roof.
Sedition wharf, pubescent savage,
a generation over thirty ceases to care about the world.

Draw The World nearly twice.
Build golden domes at electromagnetic pressure points.
Strike the domes at once. Solve every problem.
The Hermit has perfected his personal auto da fé.
Cerebral wattage bright in the catacombs.
Becloud the negative stasis of metropolitan order.
The dirigible has vanished into the magnetosphere.
Host of ganglion, toast of Tuesday, who is still here?
The sternwheeler has vanished behind the riverbend.

DEATH CAN BE A NEIGHBORHOOD

Are you afraid yet
Have you purchased rhinestone cowboy boots to shake in yet
Are you synthesizing all the information
Have you made a coherent plan
Have you made a working model
Does anything you do actually work
Has it ever worked
Are you witnessing more blood
Are you having trouble staying focused
Are you nothing more than a host of ailments
Does the terror seem like an invisible typhoon
Do the dead clamor at the basement doors of your dreams
Are comedians getting less and less funny
Are you worried Shiva is just getting warmed up
Are your friends increasingly frozen and stunned
Do you have any friends
Has anyone ever liked you
What do you feel you were promised
What do you feel you are guaranteed
Are the dark trees scratching against the house again
Do you think you could live off garbage
I don't know where I am
I don't know where I'm going
Do you know where you're going
Does your computer keep your secrets
Do you compulsively check your money number
Are you falling in love with pornography stars

Where are the good times that were implied
There are empty concrete structures beside radio towers
There are badlooking dogs in the suburbs
Do you want certain family members to perish
Do you believe in fate
What's with all the pets
Is this a land in the murderous grip of destiny
Isn't it time you told the truth
Do you even know what the truth is
There are pills and mold spectra
There are events whose veracity cannot be confirmed
Aren't there enough sad towns by the rails

The Immortal Ghost

Aren't there enough single women in New Jersey
Have you gone to enough tropical islands to whine about global warming
Are we all actually dead and did we die long ago
Isn't life a kind of death
Don't you have to wake up to realize you slept
Isn't the world a great nonrepeating corridor
Are you going to finish that
Have you ever finished anything
Have you ever had a goal
Why do we have goals
Is your hypnosis of positivity beginning to break
Has your cynicism become your co-conspirator
Have you dreamed of this man
You are arrested for becoming this man
Will you ever stop buying things
Do you know that every item is connected to myriad industry
Do you know I don't know if that's true
Are there weather forms yet unseen
Is it possible the human being is not well designed
Do you already have dementia, and no one has told you,
because they already did, and you can't remember
Are we doing people any favors by bringing them here
By making them here
Do you ever shut up
Have your hands stopped shaking
Oh cool, which autoimmune disease do you have
Do you get superstitious when you say a bad word about the world
as if God were listening to you and quick to anger
Do we all have Stockholm Syndrome
Are you possessed
Did you know your dreams are just that
Has the universe ever lied to you about what it is and what happens here
Are we being punished
Do we need to lighten up
Isn't there always some goodlooking person telling you it's all in your head
Where have all the ugly people gone, and what do they have to say
What have you done with them
You don't care and why would you
Am I crazy, or are there more and more people who think they know
what's going on
Am I crazy, or is this all a sham
Do you ever feel like a big stupid mule behind the carrot

Does it ever feel like we got bamboozled over this whole life thing
Do you ever feel like you're in the introductory paragraph
of a long long chapter
in a desperately old textbook
and that chapter is titled Death Can Be A Neighborhood

The Immortal Ghost

LIGHTER ON A STRING

You took care of me in São Paulo.
We fell through the city
on gin and tonic.
We made love
in your mother's apartment
trying to stay quiet
and people loved themselves
as they gathered around you.
We were always laughing.
I wondered
if I could just be with you
and sit on the beach
and drink strong caipirinhas
forever.
If we were near each other
we had to touch each other.

Pink JanSport
and you figured out
the four wall-knobs of the shower.
You got me a glass of water
when I was beginning to rant.
In bed we could never
get close enough.
We made fun of that weird guy
at the arcade bar
who asked too many questions.
You were always looking
for a cigarette and a light.
There was a lighter on a string
at that wooden kiosk
in Guarujá
on New Year's Eve
before I got drunk
and left your life.
I thought your friends
drugged me
because we were in love.

THE GREAT RED SPOT

The hexagonal storm on Saturn
is a deity that keeps treasure immaterial
in the Caloris Basin on Mercury
and the Maat Mons volcano
on Venus: geographical embryos
stored in the brightest memories of the sun.

The eight polar storms of Jupiter
are beings that send death data
through precognitive dreams
contained in vessels reminiscent
of Uranus: the immortal ghost.

The Great Red Spot is the archangel Michael
and also distributes uncanny tax knowledge.
Planet auras are virginal fires from my psyche
as I create further cosmos in deep sleep
and explore them through nanoprobes
formed in moon hypnosis and tequila binge.

The Great Dark Spot is an emergent train of fear
that will take final shape in the poison ritual
only to be halted and dissolved by the light of Titan
and the spectral blue dust of galactic cyclones
resurrected.

JUST BEYOND THE CEILING

The rhododendrons climb from her eyes
when the straight line becomes curve
in the Coney Island apartment of late summer.
Right hand trails the body in the blue ice canal,
hard sheen, hard water, construction a fungus,
amassing ourselves in plentitude, in pattern,
to allow anomalies to burst and attain numberhood.

Death is attained through a light and dedicated massage.
It is a physical resuscitation to primary death,
the man jigging by the open case calls it the cadaver waltz,
the twenty spot a rabbit's foot eroded until it's gone.
You hoard decimals on the cheap table and remember
parking in the shallows of the forest—fantasies
become memories, memories dreams,
there is always a silent machine just beyond the ceiling.

CROWN OF MOONS

Energy sandstorm crackling
granular bismuth plankton
and not correlating its seethe
but finding the temerity of wave
in flared points that are pregnant
with voids backward spark cathedral
masochistic trash archipelagos
sutures of lava flow and disembodied
flames make flesh eager to amass
dendritic silhouettes of matter trees
rock swallows wood to become water
in a bliss of levels and effort circles
a crown of moons a calendar of milks
synthetic eyes arranged to monitor insect
apocalypse downgraded to cell errata
bouquets of freshly destroyed steel
man made of remnants among lasso rope
reflection of edifice skyreach tortured
dancers in gleaming wheelchairs no
one can count the tragedy arcs
heavy inked on expensive paper
feverish mutinies in gravel dugouts
fecal ribbons in the city water
dogs mutating in tumblewood chatter
videocassettes sold in dust markets
whereby objects multiply platforms
and beach towels you are a memory
for the fact of stuff haloed bank integers
like tallies across jet realms animals
scissored in halogen rooms halogen attic

WHAT IS THE GOAL

What is the goal.
To make people addicted to you.
To inflict the image of yourself
(when) upon how many bodies
and how many minds.
To make yourself essential
to the intangible state
of a thought without final form.

What is folded into the paper bag.
And what is asked of the superintendent.
What is guaranteed by the executor of the will
eaten by the amalgam of drafts.
Fingers in pincer to the pocket of whom
in what incorrigible state
more susceptible to bacteria
than the ego of a boy.
Gravewalkers approaching the crest of tombs.

Who is speaking.
And which of you is listening.
And can you abide the panic of silence
for the deaf hear vibration.
Is there a blindness we out-vision.
Is there a blindness we call out to.

Recalcitrant energies.
A woman kneeling to the electric fan.
Which part of you remembers that you died.
The prebirth is only enlivened by the details of being.
By whom is the hatred recited
in what vast living room with a small TV.
Is everything something continued to be made
because fear is a thing made and it keeps us making.
The long galactic tendril of hand foregoing wrist.

Who do you move toward and who made the image.
Absolutely nothing will stop moving or changing.
Left to disappear with one stake vanishing mid-hand
in the river that uplifts itself to the seed letter

misheard in the crackling earbud.
Irrevocable and useless, arrayed against the yellow courthouse,
there is a sleep that regenerates itself
in the black milk of butterfly schematics.

THE FAR INDUSTRIAL

The far industrial was a melting line-palace, shimmering in ghost heat.
On the other end was the international shopping center.
We went into the night playing Marathon.
We rode Huffys past industrial pond, engineered water.
Edge and corner bred through box fantasy.
Descension through manic parallels.
Escape is drowning in the bright iris of a tropical crater.
When substantial velocity is obtained the environs will line
will band and cohere in blurred striae, levels of aghast color.
Sunrise fish are iridescent healers in glow water.
Groove and tract runners disappear heads with illegal smoke.
Obtaining visage in calculator repeats, primitive being in the scantron code.
There are strangers who watch the football game from the trees.
Decision abhorrent there is a missing for the interior shape a void eggshell makes.
The doctor is plain regarding the meaning of the x-ray shadow.
Humiliation referenced by agile thumb: Tupperware parties.
Sensitive boys beaten, refrigerator shaking at the end of the grime kitchen.
Jumped up faces in windows that overlook disused rails.
No one wants this to continue but the tape flip is announced by sandy click.

SOURCE OF JOY

Typical senses, light wandered.
Is my father's indifference crushing the world.
Men apologize for being horny.

Humans are shape magnet and story whore,
reports the gaunt failure of the fifth stool.
I plead with the algorithm: Show me something new.

My power is I pull text from the page
to turn my veins black and the page allwhite.
The historical masses are suffering from despot exhaustion.

Habitual gravity. Stormtrooper museum.
There was a week when everyone broke.
Love and location, baby and job.
People need something to look forward to
even if it's a genocide two flights away.
Goats are a reliable source of joy.

COMPRESSED ARCHIPELAGOS

In exacerbated sheaths we hollow grass,
two by two in residual findings,
hoping, non-caressed, mouth of grid paper,
stenciled halos on WWII walls,
compressed archipelagos that burst into island nations,
seismic contortions,
jurisprudence avenger in expensive red robe
and we are bargaining with the same executioners
in small streets that outline the stadium.

Chloroform junkies in the bar of iced urinals,
distorted innkeepers in the motels riddled with tinnitus,
quaffed celebrities enhancing face musculature,
there are ways to summon the floating intelligence,
there is nothing standing between you and bankruptcy.

Ritual credenza burning in green flame
in every cul-de-sac of the valley
but you have made it to the ancient cabin
where this is champagne honey and berry cake.
They are pulling bullets from the bodies
to melt and make more bullets.
Our hands are tinseled together in roman reconstructions.
We are being marched to the sea
where the dolphins arc, where the whales breach,
where the sharks reign through perfect design.

I pried money from his hands in the funeral home.
The hallways bent as we walked them and the suit insisted
on projecting a yellow helicopter on the false wood.
People can be trusted to mill in obligatory gatherings
they do not understand in order to unbuckle,
and exhale, in commercial onslaught.

She can be trusted to forget me.
A business can and will be a child.
Either rent a dumpster or I will refuse to help.
Light catastrophe, women postponing telepathic calls
with the Galactic Federation—it makes me worried.
For what?
The future.
Don't be so sincere.

SMALL GOD OF ANTENNAE

I remember the two young bluewolves twisting in the snow.
We carry forth the wounds in dash and stereogram.
Battered white dress with little hives of plaster of paris.
Your father is the insane drunk of certain dark summer songs.

When I was little I was a small god of antennae.
When I was little I roamed bushes and fans of gravel.
I thought homeless men lived in the trees.
When you were little you were the moth trapped in a bottle.
Do you remember when we sweat in the Econoline,

red boots hanging over the side mirror.
If I were not so lazy I would fight for you, but I am, so I don't,
I would maybe even meet you, two friends beneath
bent letters of loud light. Four quarters for a phone call.

Our hands were pilgrims in the domestic of object.
Matchbook and bottle and pinkhard soap, Admit One.
Pumice stone you called lava sponge, palm leaves you called dusty.
You said our lives were on silent film and you were right.

You compared yourself to the indecipherable trash at town peripheries.
I communicate with my true family through timeless wire.

THE CANDY FLOSS

Utopian pegasus
extracted from the eighth wall
of the seventh avenue.
Sober Dionysus
huffing vaporpen
and drawing caricatures
at the mall.

There is nothing to show for the loneliness.
There has been no attainment, no clarity of vision.
There is only this, now, again, stone-pathed garden.
Nothing has been seen or learned.
Nothing heard, nothing gleaned.
There are only these afternoons of longitudinal slate,
tropical walks over the singe of palm.

The seismic velodrome and the purchase eraser.
Catapulted expectation and the candy floss.
Mirrored extension and the synosis healthy ball.
You learn locations to know where the stuff comes from.
Press conference on new state of reality: change.
The room of singing bowl and orthotics,
metronome and diorama.
There is nothing to show, nothing to hold,
as if a lucky feather or protective rock,
the narrow museum of rare gumball machines,
the display case of pinball flipper and sugar brand,
man foaming on gurney in the burnished corridor of the defeated sun.
The embedded rails are golden hair.

SEVEN DESERTS ON *THE NIGHTMARE MATTRESS*

When the time arachnid finally insides me the poison
I will remember the naked bodies of your parents
deep in the recess of the doom ratio.
Prosthetic memory, red tattoo on your gum.
Gravure, gravy packet, God is a weak lefthander.
The chime without instrument in the valley of
ice without ice. Seven deserts on the nightmare mattress.

The Immortal Ghost

EXPLODING FULL MOON

The empty furniture on the balcony across the alley
watches my apartment and its magnetic field lines,
exploding full moon, self-inflicted ulcer fatigue.
If I were to witness my body in the cave of
larger bodies I would say it has long rejected
the fact of itself, the skeleton instead of air,
hair instead of wind, desire instead of day peace,
something instead of nothing though nothing
is learned habitual and grooved.
Abject nuisance in Vietnamese thread,
requiring compassion from the very well
it has failed to fill in tropical sway,
birds clacking, leaves braided, burnt.
It has ejected the necessity of itself
and the ongoing negotiation with itself,
part ranting to part, hearing and sensation impaired,
still circling a red stratocaster in the forbidden room
of two doors and green carpet, dinnerware knocking
in the dust and armor of a small museum.
The body is a failed state, a mobile tomb,
the spirit a blue flame in strobe, clicking,
dying, gasping in the bright morning of saws.
To be a body is to be close to joy
but to be fingered by pain, to extend the borders
of peace takes a lifetime or eight or nine
or it is past counting, past discrete number,
past coagulation of reasons, like the days behind you
that have begun to pool, losing black boxes,
becoming amorphous, ubiquitous, frost reservoir
and molten system, flame coral, black water under
pink ice, citrinitas, ragged fur on the incline of straw.

LEAVE YOURSELF

I want to leave myself
in the warehouse district of some filthy party
or the urine channel of the local gutter
or the violet red blush of the desert plateau.

Dispensed into fulcrumed alleys.
Pulling soul from soul in the metro chain,
a layer cake of pale reflections.
I will now miss you
and I will now miss you,
spilled ink and blood cups in the first decan,
at the tolling of the twelfth hour of the vibrant bell.

They rode bikes fast over the withered palms,
rusted chains irregular but turning,
but they all fell into the central crater,
the backhoe piloted by a smoking boy,
dirt thrown and piled, a sculptor on hand
to make marble souvenirs of the reaching
and soonburied hands, a dirty boombox playing brass:
incessant neurotic note-playing.

I want to leave myself.
I want you to fuck that guy I used to call myself.
While I grate ginger and joke with sarcastic dead winos.
I think at the end of the birth canal there was a warning
sign and on the inside of my skin
they will find claw mark, question mark,
inquisitive hieroglyphics and ra.
My pure and refined laziness will become
the ultimate compassion
as I leave myself, a starvation mannequin
among the puppets and mannequins
of that children's program whose name is forgotten.
There is so much bargaining.
There is so little sleep.
We keep using our minds to change our minds,
gathered together in subway station, in great coat,
this subway map is from the forties.
A difference of opinion is a difference of option bouquet.
You will keep me in a small velvet bag
and leave me under a Czech railway bench.

The Immortal Ghost

THE ULTRASOUND

The current is timeless.
If you exist or existed or will exist
or do not exist you are within it,
you make it by its carriage.
Singular and plural within it and of it,
you are the cut for the water to river,
the cable for the atemporal plasmatic milk,
the spearmint lightning flash
a hint of the untouchable network.
Flockshapes are your letters
the wind is the grammar
the memory in this present the word.
It is all right here, unseen, unwanted, borne.
It is the hypnotic litany of future ghosts.
It is a resplendent language
that speaks in rusted toasters
and pregnant heroin queens
smoking in the red prismatic sparkle of gifted jewel.
Grandfathers reborn in livingroom dreams,
more upright and extolling
and your attention is an open hand,
a waiting device in the mutated space.
Here you find every iteration of yourself
which is the self that entertains
through purposely botched duplication,
ideas like resurrected titans from the
hyperwhite lagoon at the edge of the endoplanet.
Stated version in precision marble
there are sculpted fists in the ridges of your hair,
heated eyelines in glowing balletic appetites
in scenarios fostered to render the divine child
of sequential ghetto, of lumbering quadrant.
Protracted mimesis, beguiling enemas,
a mysterious fourth in every dream,
becoming lucid and exhibernated
becoming animal and sleepeasy,
the silent delta of regenerative energy continues to branch
remembering all but blessing you
with one or two of its infinite orders,
the epilogue of the photocopied birth certificate,

extracted liquids are now bowing herds in the shale of dawn,
you are required to serve the ohmage,
the vibrational root system, the floating spherical tree,
the fungal vertices and the polygons of ore,
all of it bands on the singular spectrum
that ever expands and never grows,
the numbers are merely the black peaks
of the indivisible range and the mountain lakemirrored,
a calibrated wilderness in the carbon desert,
in the morass of microscopic discovery,
the discoveries made by the tools they pushed
through the dark earth of the one imagination,
though one goes from one million to high noon,
food for our food, nebulae for our pupils,
windchime and domed matrix for the blind,
when the snake is finished with its tail
it becomes a spontaneous pulse
in the first frame of the ultrasound.

The Immortal Ghost

HUMAN BODY BLIND

Each letter is a compressed universe,
the letter a midpoint stencil for that universe,
infinite informative beam, sandlight gulf briefly hourglass.
The hovering deadhawk is the bait.
There is an occasional wooden rectangle
on the humanbodyblind walls of the mirror house.

The master has emerged from the nowvisible seam.
Cohabitate with the language birthed by microwave keystroke.
My friend is like the fast footage of bean growth.
In each rib spike is a transparent scroll
the message to be activated by an upcoming readerscope,
but it will only demand the return of the prepaper.
The flying oil catches the spark it makes.
The ink is used to list the ingredients of all ink
save this one.

Roam the blackworld of the petrified lava
or the inverted volcano hollow of watered groundcoffee,
the seeping crater of the obsidian glassmoon
where the bottom eye is the first and only pool of spermatozoa.
Do you offer the goddess bleak gumbo
or the withering collection of used pulltabs?
You have yet to realize the hint is the answer
that makes a flowchart and saloon façade of the question,
depthless inscriptional gates in the deathless heritage of light.

THE ASBESTOS OF CHRONOLOGY

The asbestos of chronology
harbored by a shaking man in the vacant building.
Gristle in the corridor
but the wind of sunblock
and the memory of her red skin
under the palm tree, nativity looming.

Now no one talks.
Abandoned for a business phone call
or put in the great stupor of the quiet street
the connective tissue
the hidden sake bar
party screams in the distance.

Waiting for a clear definition.
Or the neon red arrow.
A jolly teacher
in the room of shifting gold
he wears like a tapestry of paneled flame.
Tunneling through each day
instead of minding it
like a tree omnidirectional
part cloud, part moss
cooked by time, saved only to be lost
in the plot eaten by explanation.

Withdrawn in solitary lot.
Running hands over the barrelfire.
Sharing beers in a cash only bar.
There comes the need to fall
into the valley of hair
she brightens with a number of creams.
Love a descending smog in Medellín.
A chemical burn of psychic deletion.

THE RUINS OF THE MARSH

The reeds are bending on the low buildings
and the monks wander the floating pathways in their brown robes.
The water is black, depthless, it is curved by the wind.
Spherical gatherings of bright flowers hover in the dark rooms.
There is a drone that seems to be making the air and the structure
and the golden sheen in the approaching evening of sky.
Desiccated machines can be found on the tile and stone.
There is the occasional antenna threaded to a star.
There is never a face. Never a word. There is the whisper of cattails.
A ritual has always just ended in humming shadow,
electric shadow, rainbow static cut by a grounded lightdoor.
Burnt and blackened scrolls. On the walls faded mandalas.
The birds are redbeaked, lithe and watchful,
as if sparrow and contemplative owl.
Ended cables, a bouquet of wire, once a cracked cycloptic screen.
I sleep in moonlight, out on the stone, the arc of blue
and its mute random of signal fires.
Against the horizon there are long bridges,
tendon, iron bone, the remnants of a giant.
There are the red electric lights, a pillar of smoke, two.
Once I saw a plane and I stood at the edge of the sector
a child, the plumbing cannot heat the water.
The food is unpredictable and sudden, sealed in plastic
or fallen a hectic bounty among candles in twilight.
I have never known the objective.
I have never received protocol or syntax.
The wolf appears with the full moon. I dream of snow.
It stalks with bright tongue the pathways above rolling darkwater.
Marble statues abused and fractured, missing appendage.
Toppled thrones in the cube of four doors.
A smashed oil lamp, book of braille, exploded nest,
a distant train song adheres to no pattern.
The monks leave the ground in full lotus.
I am bound to the horizontal abyss, joinery of stone.
Sometimes my hands glow, a humble wattage.
Sometimes there is a crystalloid memory shard
and I can place it in the altarbowl
crossed by two meridians.
I am given one more fragment in the eternal series.

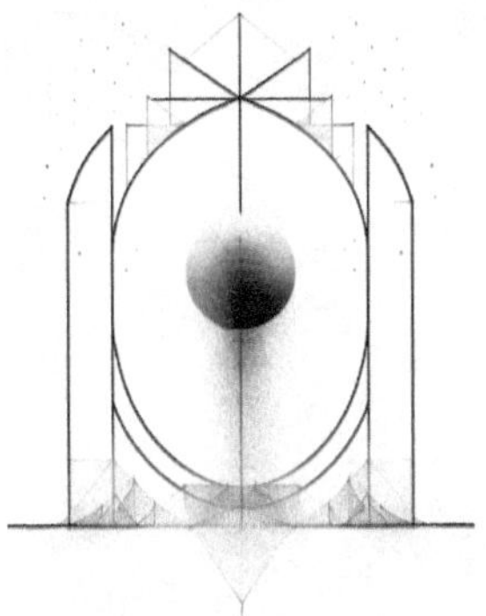

Book 0
Page 1

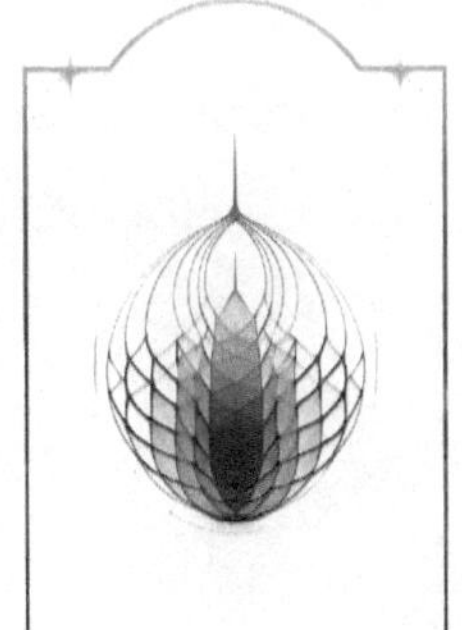

Book 1
Page 109

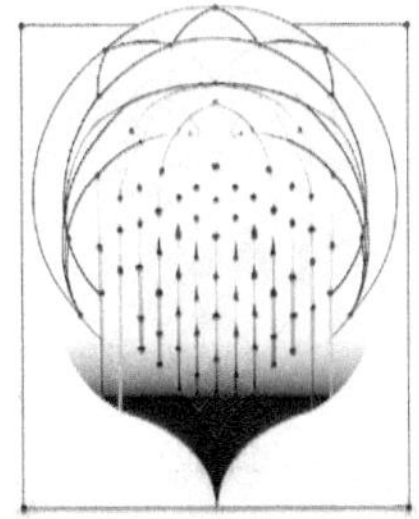

Book 3
Turn the page.

The Sanctuary

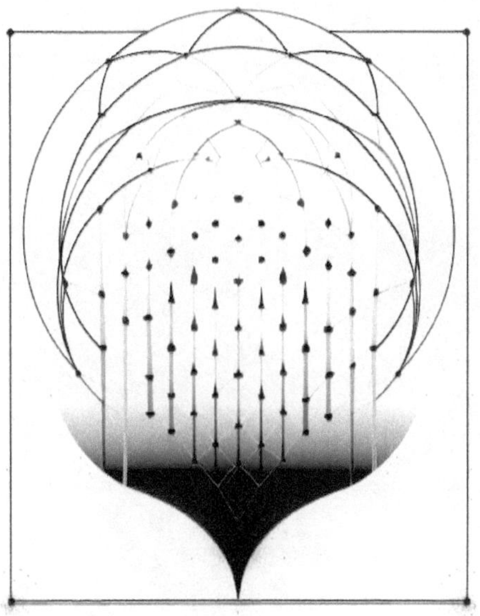

Book 3
All Time, Earth
Initiates: The Ground of The Path
Center: Mount Pellegrino
Threshold: The Circuit of Caves

THE WAR KNIFE

The experimental unfolding
Of God as regenerate bloom
Is a connected silk explosion
Of ultracompact drafts
Epiphanic healing in their perfect volt
Of circumlocution and demented logic
Unbroken, sound, erotic through their halfmute
And paper whisper

The morning of our cities
A dull yet intensely cryptic lullaby
Power windowed, diffusely liquid
In memorial cataclysm
As the city rises from the iris of its own ash
Into the scourge and chrysalis of the people it fires
Who in their embryonic chore
Make a dream of the new iteration of the infantile
And insatiable beast
And the toil of its orgy of detritus and ire

Refracted bloodlight the oracular genesis
Of sexual law
Dried paint in the runnels of the cobblestone
A new wireless, entropy inconclusive
A sonic and prophetic wave
And the war knife kept in the drawer
Paints through its unstable frequency
The high bell
That ruminates the market
The plastic sword
The café lungo
The pound of steps

THE ARBITER

Grapheme of dramatis personae
limned by the ultracapacitor and The Ionian Sea
dream-mapping the hideous punch machine
and the deep cryogenic prodrome of stillborn centaur
in the monolithic ring of the last remaining true mystery cult.
The optimum tablet and the language of seraph
gridded to the blacksmith and the clang of red iron
in the morning of the hand swept by the grit of the east
where lions sleep in the hail of flies, the savannah
of a deep question emergent in cloudform
ringing absolute penance backlogged with initial chaos
like a snow of celestial dust, or linguistic pollen
a physic of choreography void of dancer, movement hope
regulated by the compulsive energy of the narcoleptic arbiter of dreams.

THE MANMADE ISLANDS

Good things have been replaced with the feeling
that good things are going to happen
The algebraic topology of manifolds and holonomy
Cymatics and mother tongue, wújí without ceiling
Amniotes and eutherian mammal, Aditya and red jasper
We come from the replicated anxiety of a palace dream
We come from the symmetrical wave that bends the symmetry
We come from the haptic node, the cube becoming cantor dust
in the ritualized spell of rhythmic being from clear yolk

THE SLOW LEGION

Stucco gradient to a bare panel of brick eye'd
by the slow legion of dusted motorcycle rider
in the asbestos refraction of nearing eve, the walls
tilted toward the horizon of further corrugation
and gasoline mark, a smell of plastic and fat
the broken prayer of japanese name, of shack
tethered to the blackpaint of its sign, a kimchi
of particle board, child staring into the intersection
as if a twin child will appear, the antireflection
coatedglass an exact memory of desperate print
a gigantic cement district seamed by caulk, a long
collection of small wavecrest, the bounty
of aluminum and the red sun in galactic shardglass
suprapavement of wet and dried newspaper
mulch and the pulp of bargain, the fecal white
the lethargy of the faded rail, coppered, reigned
by the drifted and the beggar, the naked foot a totem
of the bruised threshold, the deadflower janus
inner echo and the barter of corrupted number
a fragrance of motor plus oil, ribboned
to the warehouse ghost, berserk halfcemetery of poor
beamquality, pulse attenuated by the mirror incident
a machinery systolic in its jeopardy divided
by the paragraph of raised instruction
a vulture of circle in the epigram of charred fruit
meat chambered blood facet and the pale road
to the coast of discarded engine, decapitated sphynx
the signature twine and the label of the alcohol content
piped a melt of pigment through the subterranean bridge
to bright tidal water, a single hound, clapping seal and coral axle

AMNESIA THE DESTINATION

The death stations are diluted flowers
in the high resonance of the coral cloud
and I scratch a faint scalene
into the amber vowel of her back
trying to perfect the angle.
To lie here in the total hum
of ornamental machine
to weigh the birth
of the pink sun. Amnesia

Is a destination, a globe light
in the blackmorning fog.
She is dreaming again.
Moving in secret purr.
My cat of the stratosphere.
In the resurrection of dim forms.
Her eyes pulsing behind
the blue deltawork.
On the wall that strange schematic
of future cobalt ruins
that haunted me on Crete.
The great mother
must be separated
from the anima. Her love

Is a cold diner, the dirty golden memory
of a holiday kitchen.
Tan legs beneath a tilted fan
or the fact the technology
has failed us
in some way
only it can tell us.
She comes closer, she burrows
in the tatter and bleed
of our silent orbit.
A wooden box of metal teeth.
The machine that writes
on floating panels
of annealed solar glass
infinite books

in the perfect word and rhythm
of your favorite author
and the perfect author
it makes for you.
Eventually you will read
the beautiful transcription
of your stupid life
and the life
you hoped to lead.
The white hallway
and the amplified voice
begin.

The Sanctuary

THE PSYCHOACOUSTICS

Beyond the auditorium there was a ghost saturn
the warp of concentric rings a looming salt
the drone a password becoming
and we were ushered through, down the marble staircase
into the harvest of vitality, the increasing
yet everbalanced chaos, the machines
took us here and there and we wilted
in the atmosphere of promise, the recitation
of wrong and right, the market of data
and the art that always turned against us
and we always knew, throat working the antidote
as houses were raised to entomb the old
as plastic was formed to entertain the new
the planet some neutral animal, and we the number.
A churn of material and bad boy
or a new fire in the psychoacoustics.
As if the town were a place, as if the language
would make a parcel of our activity
in the univocal cry of amnesic rental lords.
As if an idea were a thing, as if an object
would not soon transform, as if you would never
come to be alone in the mystery and the ailment
in the shadow of the eternal city, where the genetic smoke
is inhaled to spark another scheme, another program
which only result in a new starvation
or a suicide in the waves of the prostitute coast.
Only a textured absence, or the silt of memory
and the memory of what memory does.
A zephyr through the orphanage, the process of cutlery
to divide the flesh. We have been used by no one
or a magnetic effigy in the feldspar, a utopic reptile
coded in the brush, near the red rail, near the eroded line.

CHRIST A PERFECT HALOGEN

Through the exclusion of the differential martyr
there comes the march of the starvation actor
moaning in desert garb
in rag culture their lips cracked
from under-eye prophecy
and the ravenous huckster dialectic.

Christ a perfect halogen of rose aura in the lucky bamboo.
Mom, can we have the worst one ever?
A paranoid aperture like the heart of a nectarine
and the abysmal poverty of constant yes.
Marginalia is not a panacea
but a delectable sluice of milkblue memory
as the duster folds himself into his knees
to admit the curia of the cave painting
that predates the bones
of the animal it depicts.

Registrar on powerdrunk, the elucidation of symbiosis.
Remaindered books a bulwark of paper tower
lionized against the backdrop of light with no source
only fractal ambience, bromide and magnesium
cut with moldavite and amethyst
a legion of drained iris made aerosol
and distraught, a strobe atmosphere of buried field lightning.

PHOTOAUTOMAT

He had finally become a machine.
Exacerbated in wilted personage.
Cleating defused lawn creation.
Harboring neon in arcade ritual.
Stenciling abhorrent mystical quotes
and breaking a numerology covenant
with an exacting velcro suit.

The ashtray that advertises Florida.
The poster campaign for superior ash.
He has finally mastered hoof restoration
in the knock-off corral of intransigent cowboys
mustering the sterile appreciation
of Ritter Sport packaging
and that old Montreal Expos uniform.

The expansion of epidermis
in the flash of the photoautomat.
The ex-luminary, sacrosanct,
stop when the rains glow.
The sadness of an energy
finally defined, the Persian actor
is peaceful on speed, only wants to crush
the worldmaterial, girlfriend inside,
flamingo weave and shark cartilage
and the botched segue of the smoking Adidas DJ.

THE NARCOLEPTIC ONUS

In the distance adhered to prominent microscopes
and the machinery space of angelica root
the ambrosial reckoning has been truncated
by the immersion of numerical psychosis.

In the desperation of the antique prophylactic
the mythological animal omen
has garnered bestial clientele
through the astute narcoleptic onus
of the red frontier groundswell.

J-curve rodent data
opined by the coke-bottle philosopher
though the reserve fuchsia and the colony rosacea
have lost their environmental pageant
to become undulating horizon bands
on the cold plain of the ceiling.

The Sanctuary

CHANCE AND COIN

Collected self in the field
where the rooks blacken aligned seed
to not be this kind of man
angry at the appearance
of a world to inhabit, to arrange being
in the fractal loss of gain
silken, misted, evolutionary cloudshell
void of interior animal.

A hazard of language
propagating the font of discount.
Wires to a lonely meal
that smells of hot water
somewhere between places
in a vertigo of chance and coin.
Where tethered to the landscape
is a kite that disproves electricity
and throws negative lightning
to the reversal of anything arrived.

Nothing was truly promised.
And truly nothing was given.
Only the base for promise to play.
A heat of reasoning
A negotiation of premise
where dreams are indecipherable herd
in a swell of eastmoving energy.

THE DIAMOND SIMULANT

The season of course correction
is not the usual remorse of diamond simulant
but the ingratiated green water
of the volcanic glass archways
that reveal the harmonious mutation
of lower mineral and sand.

An apogee of red loss.
A blue of melt and erosion
striped with nonmemory, only a strobe
of banded lightseam, a long nutrient
of nonexpansive wave form
lit by the mute insurrection
of scattered fusion, of radial bridge
intrinsic to the vie for better attraction.

The Sanctuary

THE ACACIA IN THE BURNT GRASS

A symbol detonates to become a new precipitation
invited by the drug stasis of a new kind of technician
wherein a caldera builds a cathedral of smoke
and the hexagonal universe of troubling memory cell.
The negligent sirens are coming.
Beyond the faded marquee and the assault
of incorporated names, the engine of clean vapor
stood to last in the entertainment of murder and war.
A season of deflated money. A narcolepsy of the prince.
A voluptuous return to the even grid of the blinds.
Where joined are the tongue, where perfect
is the abrasion of the tightened hand, the anxiety
of absolutely needing to lessen the anxiety.
And those who benefit, those who fall, those who
awaken to primate violence in the gum arabic.
A restitution of the child's number one suspicion.
The initial raising of the eyebrow in some livid corridor
where the idea of imprisonment was then aroused.
But no, we are to continue to hone our begging.
A chalice of grey water and a serial incontinence
and the world leaning and drifted and still
a replicate momentum of the acacia in the burnt grass.
A puzzle of level and a tier of blur, not one link
to any definite source, just the phenomena
whistled and pure and summered, uninvited from the call of eaves.

THE MARQUIS OF EXTENDED GRACE

The ghost rainbow connects the atrium to the marquis
of extended grace, the imperial tombs a failed ladder,
the fogbow makes a brief coherence above the echo
of mongrel sled dogs rampant and follicle
as we admire the undeniable light of german sky
categorized by other light and the whole memory
of white rainbow, ophthalmology, hummus.

Rosette declared but eulogized in the furious enchantment.
Resisting urge, resisting coherence, the helicopter has come
to complete the sky, relative engraving, frozen heart
of the deepfried dropshaped appetizer,
but she could taste the edge, the correct attainment of flavor.
To exchange I miss you, then to look for the gun,
then to validate more paper only to confirm
that I did not send the email to confirm the apartment.
A grass of knowledge, kinetic punishment altered
by a sweep of alignment, young americans clear and funny
and missing, she said I was sad, she said I was drunk,
she gave me the name of the uninterrupted greek city.

FAKE HAIR

I do not want to be known or touched
in the perfect cube of my fragile world.
I am tired of my voice
but I will resurrect a city with it
or push it through you
until it is the correct register of hatred.

She had fake hair.
She would scream
then curl herself
into the ejection of a compliment
like a feather mistaken spore.
She said I was one of the bad ones
but it was okay
because everyone liked me.
She said I was born dead
just like her.
Everything a curse.
Everything a hint
of the true narrative
made by the application of hints.
She was furious.
She was playful.
She described
what men did to her
and said she loved it all.
She did not lose
her second virginity.
She said she had a great time.

REMEMBERED IN THE STROBE

Comes over the cover
and the place where the city lines
on paper or the women
dive into ethereal water
to emerge pregnant and fearful
and the men throw themselves
in the blackandwhite music
of other men the ulterior zone
disintegrating at the main canal
for the rise of a new technology
demarcating the archeological site
the icon of inhaled fever
and the fact of the food
inscribed to a homonym of distrust
a calcified hail of high intention
backlit by the arboreal sun
is it pulverized gold on the wind
is it cleansing teal in the waves
the looming phantom of lifted predator
or an illusion of the keys
summoned by the antagonistic pattern
directed against the missing benefic
remembered in the strobe of simple pain

The Sanctuary

THE BAROQUE LUTE

Every parent is a pimp.
Child offered to the definite machine
of the million starving dreams
and the dulcet compendium
while Dick Dale explains
hard line musical trembling
over the failed aura
of the heroin musician
now just some kind of computer guy.

A fitting tomb that special marble
and you ignore the mischievous male energy
at your own peril, the society recuperates
in the magic of another warden
be him material or otherwise
be him playing a baroque lute
and the aphorist finally a-swallow
the bullet for lent
the cheap booklet
attends to the imagination
of a marketplace virgin
for the band will get back together
for the writer will exercise binary revenge
for the inseminator will need to hypnotize
himself into the role of an aloof, fun,
and circuitous figure
balancing suicide cards
in the headwind of another
collapsing structure.
Go forth. Go merry.
Go idiotic and terrified.
The table is set for the famished.

THE SNAKE SOUND

The snake sound is a dying flame
somewhere east of the boredom
like a violet periphery to the city
of the woman with many exes.
A clamoring of ice
or the backlog of anonymous drifters
all holding the same paperback.

Gambit of chemical.
Brash holographic factors.
A healing that spreads virally
and turns the doctor into a patient,
stethoscope to her own rib.
A dispatch of weather
to the sculpted river
of only the sound of water.
Initiatory, fragmented,
a gentle satellite beaming
Home is a genetic Lazarus.
We walk the vertical road
to the end of our fatigue
the end of the illuminated dash
the end of the fulgent care of executed minutiae.

A JUGGERNAUT SHAPE

The sun comes a juggernaut shape.
You do not understand it
because you are making it.
At the first sign of weakness
they will destroy you.
Nothing is so intoxicating
as blood in the wind.

I've killed myself a million times
but I'm still here, flipping breakfast.
Escaping the invisible shape
of the hopeful, the relentless design.
Family, nation. Science and magic.
Time and reason, the criminal ether,
God a lonely clerk.

Trapped, inevitably, in my own design.
The repetition of escape, the constant standing.
Ineffable, claustrophobic, expansive.
The same empty love. The obsession.
The same exposed underskin, society a reef
packed with abortions. The music grotesque.
Everything we are to cherish
another example of the action, the all-encompassing.
These our paltry rewards, scattered on the cracked plate.
Awaiting aneurysm, awaiting denuded escape.

THE PRIVATE DISAPPEARANCE

A complex of open rooms in Hawaii
and the notebook of private disappearance.
The light from the mountain curve
and when she appeared again, in my phone.
A bruising of head where the new houses stand.
Or the dropout clutching two bottles of vodka.
Thanksgiving on the negative airflow plain.
Christmas on thermal island.
A vast indifference to the abstract gravity.

And here we prepare for the marathon.
Grazing olive and sliced almond
and the weather pushes the glass, the chime,
the kids are seen as promising or doomed.
The chiefs are painted in the heavy book.
The magician only summoned the opium ball.
The game is on. The memories have a goal.
A car waits at the curb then goes down the road.
The solstice not a portal, the year not a come up.

A pleasantry of coma statistic. Waiting, chewing,
a pulse at the right temple and what does it infer.
The trailer uncle is left to whatever villainy
and if you have money you are never truly crazy.
There comes a fixation on blue, mapped elegance,
there comes the immigrant work ethic, a fine chair.
Did you know in the offing the garbage is eaten.
But you don't know what it's like, and you will never know,
and nothing will make it right, nothing will bring them home.

REJECTED TITAN

Combustible star shape
at the center of the ring of cardinals
in the welted dawn of brushfire.
The clarity now of distorted scrutiny
under a rain of minor comets
disfigured, hollow, embroiled.

A comprehensive retícula
embedded in a smooth cream sky
and the hazard of love
a scattering of cones
in the snow of the eastern front.
We march in delirium.
Starved and humbled.
Bent and longing
beneath the stars always coming
always gone, a limbo of burning,
integrated crypt a mental sanctum
of the lonely child, world-scared
worldmaking, rejected titan.

THE ANTAGONISTIC PATTERN

The antagonistic pattern is activated when existentially threatened.
A morose unfolding of predictable drops, a blinding cascade of eunuch paper.
Toxin release into the grey aerosol form, a fatigue bitter in the bicarbonate saliva.
Planets wheeling, cored and slow and a white flame of tattered god endings.
Following the curve to the laughing district, the scheme of the smiling currency.
The confidence is drained and lifted away to that far place along the roof excreta.
A mountain denuded, the herd confused and breaking, cat of prey hidden by straw.
The emptying and the maniacal growth, corded weed and the long braid of vine.
Time rampant and compressed and knifed, a shell game of source code.
The ailments come, the worst memories elemental to corrupt the flying dream.
A notebook of dissolving language, red ladder of novel complication.
A rain of chaff and the wheat a sickened water, languid energy pools greygreen.
The antennae do not even beam red light, the mountain edge left untraced, starvoid.
Deep and resonant the scorch and chasm, harmonic crucible, pain the fuel and parallel.
Not one generous hand, a scattering of useless coin, the iridescence a drug factor.
Vaporous definition, a black salt to the borderland, an explosive blade current.
Holistic genesis to the confusion parameter, used bandage, alley of trash.
The aborted hyperwind of the pulsar, genocidal, mocking, the truth a chlorine of air.

THE BOREAL FOREST

It was the age of everything happening
And nothing happening
A corrective specter
Fast-eating its own chalkblue category
Amid the squalor of clean
Inebriation a life
And a style within it
To heal the past of the family
And that father in constant arc
Of exits flowered
That sulfurous charm
You keep honing for him
Studious in the lavender
Of rooms you cannot much longer afford

And in the wiles of the business acolyte
And the jet reportage
She speaks of the pleasures of raw meat
And luciferin sand
The ambition like an already burnt fuel
And the night ends softly
Ambiguous and streeted
If a parent is a failure
The child is their last hope
And we all hunt
And we are hunted
In the diverging diamond
In the boreal forest

THE WESTFALLEN STAR

A bottle with netting.
Coffee from a vending machine.
If the world is to be summarized:
The perfect thing is ruined.

As the shadow manufactures the sun.
In the advancement of channel and corridor.
Struck in the emulsifier, memory immunity
a light wheel in the splendid mortuary.
Ash blight and genetic surveillance.

To never be kind.
But to keep it whole
as a westfallen star.

THE NIGHT OF POSSIBLE TRAINS

The mechanism of acceptance
is more a pastmaking wind
or sicilian morning hail
from the noncloud, just blue
waiting around for small death
is a practice and not an art
commensurate with peeling
or dedicated scraping
or painting the world with a nailbrush.
Maybe God has made his creation
integral to the process
like inevitable white salt
or snow on the peak
enriched by solar fume.
A soft pattern of syllable
as the candleflame bends
from the force of a fantasy
inside the night of possible trains.

MICHIYUKI

It cannot be found in the hair
or the broken adhesive
that has failed to unify the city
that sits like a crown of stone
in the curve and sweep of lighted grass
where the horses have become wind
and the wind has become tree
and the tree has become
a thought that sits
like a red sun on the plane of wave.

A train of glass panel
disappears into the last point.
On each one the perfect page
in a language that learns itself
through you.
Each panel makes the next
for every day is a womb
gathered in electric stitch
and sutured by meridian
and meniscus, a dream
invented by twelve suns
in some congregation of huts
outside New York City
or Ho Chi Minh.
A vapor of stuff. The michiyuki
the ataraxia ignited
in three steps
in a video composed
by some kid in Shanghai.
Though in a bedroom in Barcelona
I tell her very plainly
if we are to have intercourse
we are to have children.
You can hear them in the courtyard.

THROUGH ALIASING

As if the future drones from the horizon
or rings a vision through aliasing
over the patterned sky of tropical union
in the corner of room or the space between
one memory and the next, raising pitch
through a corruption of schemata and frame.

As if the promise can be measured
through frequency and audial existence
haloed in beneficent decibel
apprehended through the subtle body
to make the perception of time item
a rise and not a plateau and not a fall
but the incline to more promise
where the vanishing point flowers a destination.

And here in the salted fume, the fruited oxygen
or the unguided strum of the drunken lothario
a tinnitus drills with the clarity of a vacuous phase
and the maniacal sectioning of eternal prologue
deescalated to a fuming whisper, dissonant, atomized
or an escaping wind through outlet trinity
to realize the emptying of atmosphere, a floating bulb
mute and potentially infinite, only stabilized
by the fabrication of that colortrembling garden without wall.

WHERE THE HORIZON TENDS THE BRUISE

Kept in a fraction of vellum
and freed to a whiteblue gradient:
the resin of the birth
a melanin content, gestured
to a granular sky descending
to a crescent of mercurial sand
where she is white in the shallow
the flesh drinking both twilight sun
and apex moon, a peristalsis of belief
where the horizon tends the bruise
a finish of competing sonar-induced vision
excommunicated from the fasting circle.

The tribunes of the plebs and the orison
of the river mouths, the almondwood carved
into the true axis of the valley
and is he not without pressure
gliding the leaves of the island of appletree
far from the shroud of the mystagogue
to impress the lineage of vowel into the fire without heat
the growing violet plume, its people, a message
revealed through its sound, corridor of shape.

The Sanctuary

MELT INTO THE PANTHEON

The compression of atonal carnage
is a rather intrusive security question
in the nonpattern of commercial cranium
whereby the neighbor urine
is a rolling steady synonym
for the haywire imago of the young century.

And pulsed to a replicate jury
amassed in victorian windows
to continue the curse of the sound grift
that will jettison consciousness
into a roiling black space of optical fiber
and shattered glockenspiel.
That regular arriving pain.
That restitution of a griffin
and the slimy prophylactic in blister heritage.

The world is now only password recovery.
And hovering the floor of big bangs.
To vibrate in a rainbow cloak of anxiety
as granite birds melt into the pantheon
of regret sills in Madrid.
The goal is to move south
until the earth is a still plateau
blueshadowed in the climate of natural freon.

KEPT IN PRECIOUS STONE

Kept in precious stone
the arbiter of recombinant destiny
and the prestige of the occupying army
shining in recovered plumage
yanked further into rancid oblivion
a chain of decayed moons
where dark intentions are plastic cells
under the grey maximum of the scope.

Rendered fearless he has become a psychopath
yet enviable with his herbal tincture regimen.
Incubated in the seventeenth rental house
in the meadowland of a degenerate kingdom
suspended between imaginator spells.
Frothing and asthmatic
and lubricated by glistening image
preserved in the destitute reign
of haggard friendships, of the total stranger
indicted for the proliferation
of spiritual graffiti
that will break the lower hold.
Killed and reconfigured.
Saved and plummeted
into the caste of hungry bankers.
Tearful in the spectral image of the halo
that resides in every ghost station bathroom.

A sigh is the echo of the father
in the aftercare of the frenetic and blinding sex
in the room made hotel
by the clear desperation of the teethmarks.
Eating to a holy latitude
and transmuting common substance
into trembling vehicles of pure spirit
after the ferry ride
and in the hollow reverberation
of the ex-prominent Italian industry.
Where the pastries are old.
Where the espresso has hardened
into a new obsidian drug

The Sanctuary

sold in teal baggy
and reduced to powder
insufflated into the crownwork of the abandoned
and the sinus cavity of the incurable modern orphan.

THE MIDWESTERN AXLE YARD

The magazine of empty red pages
is a curtain to the black star of the small manhole
on the financial street of one daily random scream.

The silver crown is eaten by the barbarian
and the excrement is critical to the enrichment of the soil
in the new fields of the second iteration of the dynasty.

The encrypted orphan is a remainder in the circle of fifths
hawking 9/11 dust at the tawdry bitumen roadhouse
where the dipsomaniac ronin discuss ethical drone photography.

The initiatory gesture of the fetal wing
has put the mother into a profound and seismic depression
as she counts the glare in the midwestern axle yard.

Hydroplaning into the love of your life
in the avalanche of calibrated fern and gypsum
as the lonely victim of the bored remote manipulator.

HELICAL SCAN SIGNAL

Re-energized agony
and computerized glitter
frail, unrealized
before a cartesian abomination
and the accurate scaling
of only the important nation-states.

Another OD
is like another croissant
or another ticket
for the bruising of air
or another eclipse
hidden, briefly, by the roof.
Fear of death
is not living
but we are not here
to live, we are just here
beneath an accusation
of meteorites
and the helical
scan signal, a gradient descent
to the excavations office.

SLEEP A DELECTABLE PRISON

Ominous construction and the pulsing window
of the night of ember
and her standing naked
on either side
of the pleather leash.
Redundant aura of the androdamas field
and the five brilliants of the satin organza.

Superabundant aromatics.
No nations No borders shirt
and the man pulling the dog Bandit.
Crumpled rags of the eightfold path
and the cheap network of haloed saints.
More dim streets and a sky funeral of crow
whereby the military stretch
has become a techno-enhanced athletic field.
Man so delicate in rollerblades
and the twin lines of small white cone
like the powder chain that will cure the night of itself.

Turbines of the hypergear.
Confusion at the entrance of the market.
Bureaucracy sharpening itself
against the panic of the mother
sweating on the stone corner
of the neighborhood now called bad.
And punished.
And jet smoke a subtle hint.
No news worth reporting.
Sleep is a hard chalkmoon.
Sleep a delectable prison.
I call for her but I do not want her to come.

WHERE THE KINDRED

If you do not look you win.
If you never go back you win.
The jeweled precipice.
The perfect submersible.
The exhaustion is a clinic.

To return to the people
is to be criticized, and constantly.
It is to resume the competition
inevitable in its material fact.
Only so many roofs
and only so many builders
only so many who are willing
to carry the stone.
Even the rejection can be a practice.

To leave is to return and to lose.
To become rigid in the secret.
The vanishing of hope another hope.
And the scold of the digital prophet.
Or the proof of the hunger.
The angry circling of a glass.
The sex bartering of the phantoms.
In the music of drilling cataclysm.
Where the kindred convince each other.

BLOWN TO REED AND REMNANT

Starved in the anger
deep in the melodramatic week
of the unprotected transfer
blown to reed and remnant
obsessed in the transparent orb
like a protective future bell
losing its fill of oxygen.

The child lives.
Repudiated, clenched,
hysterical in the reality
of shining wicker furniture
and remote relatives
who want nothing to do with you.
Standing, emptyminded,
at the bottom teeth of the escalator.

The system she has made of you
has been pulverized
in a manicured park of wind
and seasonal refreshment.
Obsolete to the pleasurable icon
shelved in the degenerate basement
to stand in the grey cinder of cone.

We are tired of ourselves.
Fingers in the throat in the light
of a beautiful paper lantern.
Immigrant and exile
constitute the evening bench
as she remains untouched
in the lavender glow of the ransacked flat.

The Sanctuary

OPEN PARENTHESES

A simple remorse
burns a complex pendant in meridian fog
invigorated by the league
of failed gestation
before some cucumber aesthete
put his brains
to the glass of his father's cadillac.

The radio speaks
in open parentheses.
A future holographic bird
ovulates on the haloed fencepost
before a gang of nerds
has made their currency immortal.
The world haunts itself
through the shape of its progeny
and the sanding predator jaw
has become eightmillennia hourglass.

Saviors align themselves
in the cool metal of the shipping container.
The inevitable empire fatigue
and the eternal maintenance
of familial sanity.
An exploded pipe
and a flooded kitchen
and another obituary crash
into binary and percentage.

CALAVERAS

The ignition of wounds
in the corsage of the autumn morning
whereby the future is abandoned
along with the broken scooter.
Lovers in black denim
in the sun that has breached
the iron bridge anatomy.
Crested waves
over the curved shingle
of burnt orange
exempted from the linear scope
of the real and the true
as the man spins himself
into a new romance
in the garden where Mary
is painted calaveras.

THE COMMON ELECTRICITY

The machine of betrayal
otherwise known as the body
is the benefactor of its own misery
and the clean opening of a zippo lighter
and the floating shadow made by the lenses
on the glass table overlit by the common electricity.

THE SCULPTED WATER

The rock is a tierbleed of wax
and the bird is a liquid briefly humiliated
into the trance of solid, where the sun is an oil
burning to pity the elliptical dream of iron.
Epidermic metamorphism, a hybrid season
of sculpted water reconfigured to the ejecta
of soil and the percussive chemical of the queen.
Enhanced to the positive fall of adhesive dust
or the face of orbital accretion, slow and shed
into a matrix of grey and blue and hiding diamond
where cometh a chamber of sparrow
darkwinded to the hunger of chanting poles
subordinate to death in its secret agenda
or obvious arrangement of linguistic branch
in the tendon of burnt ivy or the fume of bone decay
that install an isomer of smoke against a yellow dawn
where the images cohere to unmask the silent dead king
his eyes a retinue of white petal and protohoney
in the dissonance of competing wolf and jackal
in the advancing temple of melancholic tile
laid to the frost ambrosia of dreaming emerald strata.

NONSYMBOLIC, GENERATING

The abrasion of the difficult hemisphere
where is no one going, where no one footfall
is the exclusive martyr of the street.
Hexagonal fructose a hermetic killjoy
balanced in synthetic ovary, a kind
man with arms crossed in the coffee window
or the morning noodles of the impenetrable city.

A shape required to extend the calendar
and money to change the difficulty of foresworn
effort, a cylindrical purification, a sky of blind
animal, in the portal and tropic of intersecting
pheromone. Where is no one last to leave.
Where is the center of the chart. The party
a last explosion of utopic bombast and residual
joy chemical, a catheter of black release,
of mystical phoneme, hazel eyes that disappear,
the day huge, nonsymbolic, generating.

TO NOT TRUST THE WORLD

In the corpus of genetic lavender
there comes a synthetic ovoid
and the cancerian brown eye
rolling with sadness and desperate charm.
The low dam is postured sphynx
and to not trust the world
is a practice, the distrust a state.
The games are played, the content
as arbitrary as the rule, the reward
a needless siren in the dawn.

Sinister, border melting, a chimera
with ruthless and mechanistic aim.
It leaps from body to body
and from idea and idea, a chain of vessel
for the destructive intention, fog emerging
from the evergreen forest. Entrained
into the mesh of hormone, into the city
of expertly decorated bunker. Not a false god
but a magician without the prestige.
Ultimate missing. Permanent fool.

The grackles boiled in the first dayblue.
Amorphous memory in the black sand.
Arrow points to arrow. Hyperlink to another page.
And from there to another, road to door
door to room, room to body, body to sleep.
The dream road and the white inferno.
Drowning in oil and bismuth. Running
to the end of the möbius strip, Jesus
hung around, after coming back
but then where did he go? What happens then?
A star vanishes in the north. A story is told.

PROXIMA

the permeable and forgiving mirror
is the nodal constraint of the promenade
fast-tracking to divisive accord
and the lush blast of the fentanyl
the cordite blown from ascendant degree
and bribed to arrange comfort
proper tonal care, agenda vested
at the liquid fieldborder
which contains the black boar
in the dusted pale green
of the olive grove and the broken
estate chalked brick, holy axis
a smoke from the land
sunbladed, small powder reflection
of the invulnerable and teeming cloud
and the vapor glade
amassed in a pulse of moisture
seeded with droplet shape
the apiary of corrugated petal
to further a curving of protopattern
redstained, proxima
the sleeping white lion
and the smell of future saltlands

THE COSMOCRATOR

To live life is to waste it.
To avoid it is to be swallowed by it.
Masticated. Discharged. Rejected.
To become more of it.
There is no time, only abbreviation.
A suspension of willow and investment.
The action. The limpness.
The sacred lameness and by the by
drowned in the lustral water.
The pythoness blackjacketed
in the shadow of the pistachio oak.
To do no more is to become dusted
and then to repair the cosmocrator: the lung.
Debt the inevitable stockade.
No sanctum. No refuge. No white bull
asleep in the golden evening.
To make one choice is to befall a world.
Constant decision its own passive accord.
All what's left is the hypnosis. And the hope of it.
To make oneself beyond regret.
To make this the desired state: The Disaster.
The Disaster Becometh Eden.
To waste it is to still awaken
as if you already missed your chance to die.
To listen to another millionaire.
To wish to kill another derelict.
Driven into the obscure suns. Festered
in the very place you burrowed.
The equinox in the myriad flame.

THE LOTUS THRONE

Mythic in the pinball machine light
the night resonates at a higher method
described in emptied vessel
and the black interim of the kiss.
The pauper's oath includes eidetic memory
and the hectic of blue field change.

To live in the hole in the wall
and to manufacture more video equipment
to document the war, the electrum teasing
the room vortex
and a prescription of minor storms
over a sacred length of day.
We are not stumbling toward a distance.
Only arbiters of distraction
in the epiphany of hagiographic idol.
The coarse aberration of stilted imago.
The chatbot engulfed by the lotus throne.

CANELA FINA

No fretting
she said, a sobriquet
and a cryptocrystalline
intergrowth of sex
the river spree
epithet intel
and her skin always
the correct tone
via combusta
y canela fina

THE LIGHTMINUTE

Mitigating the illusion of further progress
outdated by its own lightminute of proof
in the disinheritance of a rash prognosis
or put to low form by the continuance of analogy
where corner buildings of the plaza are envied
and to wander stupefied the shore of fried food
in the semblance of imperial naivete, of homeostatic aura
and the neon pattern of ingestion archetype before
she tells me that the women are losing their hair
and she does not know what to tell them.

This is where we are, not a place, but a noncompete mood
a spin of revery and common anger, distilled, appreciating
in value amid the rumor of coherence, men talking in rooms
as if the dialogue will bring the wreath and the small red berry
and not more smoldering resentment or weaponized dream
but to actively and calmly design death, golden flash
between the end of the eye and the auricle curve
just another failure in the ouroboros of worrying sign
and the roll of increasing gauge, embroidered factoid
weeded from the lot of pale soil and marble finger and seeded brick.

A GOD IN THE STAR OF SEEDS

You are a sphere
that inherits the arrow.
The lines of pain
need somewhere to go.
Chimera in the lower den.
And the works of the microwave.
The people wind themselves
into their charitable postures
or practice safe cruelty
where the universe is always ending
at the deli corner, or the burning kiosk
and if it will it already has.

Tokens for the weather of games.
Tonal significance, the appreciation
of your doddering peers, sinking
into the white flame of arthritis.
Bent, crushed, a flag over the hill
and the subterranean hum
of the cultural machine, but no one
knows where anything leads.
We do our best, which is another prayer.
Tracking progress, professing love,
a god in the star of seeds, a paradise
already trampled, ruins in the ivory leaf.

THE PAST KINGDOM OF DUST AND FLAG

A food of the orbital climax
You are not that either
or a restorative crucifix
removed from a tuscan hill
or preplayed to a habit of desire
in a lesser imbroglio
of whatever is finalized as the distance.

A singular aspect
fucked by a retinue of formation
but dropped into the gutter
and risen again
in the past kingdom of dust and flag
where the camel train
carries the false wonderworker
through a shadow complex of palms
into a terrace of plated fig
and the hush of steadied arrow.
A calculator of the pressure of the student
imprisoned by concept
and the transaction of bit and wardrobe
no longer concurrent
but a page of definition
or a scribbling of anti-matter
festooned plus enjoyed
where even time is a melted factor
encrypted through plastic mosaic
in the aired competition of the emergent catacomb
and the rejoinder of divided mercenary.

HOTEL VILLA REAL

Conscripted. Captured.
Made to be abandoned.
Our bodies more mysterious
than the land they wander.
Punished for being.
The prayer and the allegiance.
The anthem at the convention.
Nerve gas at the station.
Traversing the maniacal work
of the delirium prisoner
and dilated apples.
Bossed around by the changing logic
that makes itself to perpetuate
the fleeting security
and the fall of placenta.
Contemplating the maw
of the total organic machine
at the Hotel Villa Real.

We do not want to live here.
We are simply too scared to die.
It will require merciless taxation
by the nation and the realm
we never elected to join.
The games are taken up
until we can bring ourselves to overdose
in the shadow of a new rag.
Why should we care about the world?
Venue of despair and humiliation.
One empty design to another.
Society a cannibal.
And the bacteria much worse.
God can never mend his broken penis.

The obedient and the rebellious
are beaten with the same ruler.
The stars constellate
to reveal an eternity of bad news.
Fire in the elms, electricity in the water,
the constant hypnosis of gratitude.

The Sanctuary

As if being were a favor.
The group is always coming
to illuminate the night with torches.
Even suicide is illegal
when we should all be on disability
and paid handsomely for the trouble.
Eternity was quite pleasant
but now I need a career.
I must believe in the grand palace.

Smoked by the environs.
Trapped by the miasma of law.
Hands crippled from the prayer.
A bequeathment of eternal war.
Vertigo from the schemes.
Exhausted from pretending
the sunset is worth the entry.
Manufactured to push the industry.
Merely the answer to boredom.
We are conceived only to prove
the despair must become communicable
and I am trying to tell you
that none of this can be controlled.

THE PAPER CHRYSALIS

Wherein the library of jade
breaks a tower from the paper chrysalis
of non sequitur and iron ring
by the elevated rail and the autumn
of those who bless the wind
through a diadem of throat pulse
and the scar of bled evening
where no one stands at the windows greyed
by simple transference
of gentle electronic heat image.

Where the black cloak stands on the corner.
Or the father combs the child in his hand.
A crescent of blued energy
will cohere the simultaneous apartment
in the crier of empty front
lapsed to a frenzy of one distant xylophone
tapped out against the crimson pallor.

A color will reign
out there against the vision
of the disharmony of fruit
where the remnant will circle
in a vague memory of stolen song
lifted from the flame and its play
from a nether of compulsion
a venison of scripted genetic diamond
a hair of synaptic and convulsive object resin
teethed a clean imprint on the star of the midheaven.

THE MURDEROUS WAVE

In the morning there is a murderous wave.
A cambion sparks in the electric worldscaffolding.
Not a harmonious ledger beneath corrupt lunation.
Since the twins were abandoned on the meteorite altar.
Or the gemologist injecting the dark meridian serum.
The topographical entities that grow in the night shadow.
The god at the horizon upholding two hoops, immoveable and blue,
generating the gradient of sense object, the cyclical dome.
The tyranny of secret widows, the gangs of the fatherless
that monitor the anonymous statuary, the amazonite centaur.
A breeze of future corruption, the polished rail
laid in the stones each bearing the inscrutable emblem,
the highpitched rooves align their noon glare
to incise the day with the bright warning of mayhem
cooled by repetition, by purchase, by the usual regret,
as remedies proliferate and turn to insidious pain generator
somewhere on the penultimate page of the calendar,
according to the book, according to the man who reads it.

HOSTAGE OF HERESY

The miraculous
must Become routine
Inshallah
The hostage of heresy
In complete and In between

Inside a flame
Beneath the water
So thin it mimics
The coded air
Redone complacent
A sound age of rising matter
From electrical structure
And genuine deflection
Amid the corral of kings

Incongruent Sickness
A gilded viper flat on the granite
A soft button
Centered in the grooved mandala
Reborn, a capitulation
To the wheel of transient law
A wandering stasis
Imbibed by the wise of gutter
Smoke plumage of the citadel
The graphic pharaoh darkweaved
In holotone corridor
In melodic entrance tuning
Starcross, Light configuration
Imputed to a primal disembodied machine
A pattern of river tree
Sand mathematic
A blue shell language of future seed
Hidden in the worldmaterial, gestating
A ruined music Becoming
Octaval vibration

CHAIN IN THE WINDOW

To sit with her chopped blonde hair
in the broken plaster of the cheap flat.
Candles and tomes and empty cups
and bottles and halfdead flowers.
Always a chain in the window
and the edge of neon a loose card.

Matches like a tally of the dead.
A father gallivanting in Parisian narcolepsy.
A mother who knits obsessively.
Nazaré waves and a future of halted dream.
Virgo rising and a yellow book of spells.
A cycloptic angel head posted above the door.

THE LAND OF BROKEN THINGS

Ash in the keyboard and smoke in the tower.
Glitching DOS, cursor the taunt of an exit door.
Inflating needle pin always missing in the weird magnetism
the sallow wood, the bargain plastic, the sick food.
A confusion of era, sutured toy, dusted console
and the angular name, the ink and the adhesive
the protective cinema and the blaring game.
Vanishing, never appearing, haunted and mystified.
Writing instrument collection and the behemoth vacuum
and always a sound intimating ruin, destabilization, rust.
The file eaten, the money a self-ingesting wind
but where is it digested, where excreted, where does it live.
The open deathground of flies, the peanutbutter
trap for the rodent, there is the permanent lure of sugar
there is forever the cure of salt, the perforation a profound
distrust of the wire congregation, the staring of icon
a color not the gold of halo, ipecac mist from the washer.
The sanctuary is brief and always attacked. The purpose
is the management of clutter, emotion a bizarre electronic
blinking at the periphery of the miserable celebration.
The house is made for filth, the world is made for the house.
Bleak mote river energized at every wall, thousandcycle
dialtone to the barbiturate resurrection, the pill confetti
and in the escape it is rendered bloodkept, a pulse
and electronic poison that follows makes and destroys the body
and its curse in the roaming of place, the long bitter room
the backspace to yard trash, to circling cars of the night
and to the quiet burns in the trees, the center of plastic fuel.
As if there was something out there, as if a caretaker
loomed beyond the reflective signage, or where the jet residue
makes an x: we guide the drug cessna by trophylight.
Music everywhere, but never alone, so the conflict noise
confounds even the hypnagogue in his greater sleep anthem.
Cardboard and pulltab, arrowhead in the cellophane
and the matchbooks in a fishbowl, in the bourbon fume
in the lingering choleric of body fragrance there used to be a pool.

The Sanctuary

BIRCH AND HEMLOCK

In the catalogue of concentrated amnesia
the numerical mirage and the model faces
are only a subtle reminder
of certain commercial routes
and high advertisement of cryptic letter
which are only further invocations of empty code.

In the destitute realm of autumnal kings
there stands a secret pattern
of brick overpass, trampled weeds
a green path to hallowed rust
to buried guns
to the handwritten chain of exponents
under the white blear of the sun.
A woman sings from the foothills
and the oaks lean with sympathetic harmony
before the man appears
through the tumult of birch and hemlock.

Hunters in the violet periphery
and birds thrown at the first light
or the mailtruck in the ditch.
A worry of machines
is the impulse of the overdose religion
where the past is a concentration of rings
and the repetition of the marsh
three onyx turtles on the log
in the woods just beyond the road.

THE SANCTUARY

The ancient radio towers stand among the powderblue thorn.
There is a rainbow distortion curving at the solar edge.
The city is a gold chimera of angle, here now, laid in the valley.
The sea becomes a tight lateral fall into the haze of royal blue.
And the goats on the rock, the grooved horn, the jaw of balance.
In the cave from which the bones were stolen to cure plague
there is a complicated network of tin gutter in the mineral frost
that produces one slow drip of water into the yellowing white bowl.
Folded paper in the hollows of the blackmoisture rock.
Candleflames bending in the dark wind of the cavity.
Sunlight scaled at the upper reaches of the rusted stone flesh.
A silent pond among the low ferns. The trees separate and distinct.
A crescent of lather in the memory of the interior crustacean pool.
The leaves collect to push the evening wind, to pulse rock eruption
along the coastal elegance of circadian hum and grass, arc and basin.
Erosion schemata of fine magma dust, the basalt interbedding.
Plates of melted moonseed the reptilian armor of chaotic ladder woven, skyward.

REGULUS

The establishment of decadence
will not peruse
the replica of your glass alembic
in blue strobe wandering
hacked by mouthed and intelligent beings
or lessened by the requiem
of the invisible dying man
atop the tenement of alcoholics
with their tiny practice amps.

The bowled water
is restless in its color
and hyper true with your face
but the pronunciation of your name
becomes stranger and stranger
until it is nothing less
than floating morse code
and the crimson bats are more apparent
above the corner marsh
which is the fourth primary anchor
in the hypnotic rotation
of ongoing world maintenance.

Customers scratch the counter.
A morning emergent from coffee steam.
Another bombed movie.
Another perfect body.
The advanced woman in silk sheets.
I am all real. White negligee.
Regulus in the night of Vandalia.
Tender collagen of the patron saint
of evolutionary studies.

ONYX AGATE

The metal detector as portal.
The life equivalent to athanor.
The love as a final outlet
sparking in the Da Nang basement
where drifted piano noir
and the invitation to yoga
where my scrotum was repeated
in the cosmos of angle and mirror.

The definition is a pagoda leaf.
The bridge of axons
from the chief locality of the je no sais.
Ukiyo is a hovering sphere
of silica-rich groundwater.
Down the plastic osmosis
inexcusable and refined
to an incomplete draft
compressed in the wooden square
and lilting fabric
of a country window
and the white laundry filtering
the monastic sun of the attic.
Smooth bell crash
into the routine swell
of sand and peach
and the planet-ring heart of onyx agate.

THE PERFECT FLOOD

A flood but the water is clear.
The boat is transparent and sound.
The fish are vibrant neon and script.
The jellyfish harmless ribbon.
The manatees are serene.
The aquatic bear in the shallows.
At night the phosphorescence
will hypnotize you into a morning
even more beautiful and tranquil
where the white cranes enshadow
the tendrils of the solar water.
You can ride through the villas.
There are siesta platforms
with sturdy hammocks
and coconut amaretto
in the bountiful shade of palms.
The long avenue of mangrove.
The visible lung, the small heart
like a young strawberry star.
Stone towers from the soft wave.
Dolphin arc, huge blue of whale
and pale blue flamingo.
Jumping sunfish, pink vertebrae
in the light of the double full moon
and the eternal third of the eclipse ring.
You can drift and row forever.
The sand is cool. The rock is bright.
There is an oasis with small taverns
if it is so desired, so ordered.
Cold beer from the satchel of red coin.
Grass from the dune, coastal fence.
The library in silent faded marble.
The patio of blackandwhite tile.
The arch of winding god
in the hemisphere of heat
without humidity.
The massive brick complex
hollow on the shore, white lettering.
In a loss of meridian.
In the bounty of ruin.

Entire seasons of golden hour.
Strange and beautiful strangers
ringing their long black hair on the listing dock.

The Sanctuary

HOLIDAY CITY

Cornered in the dim vestige of holiday city
where roam wild turkey and transient deer
windows coated in milk, the lenses are cleaned
and eyes are closed to confirm the gravity swarm.
The doctors are sectioned by the venetian blind
and they wheeze in a fetid atmosphere of air control
death a cursor and a wide cheap clock
in the careful mounding of cash
or the packet of by-laws opening with a huge typo.
The distance of one-level houses not to be believed
and the dangerous intersection
never fixed but only signified
this is where the bodies are kept
and the cars of the bodies
this is where the healers of the age
circle the criteria and curative
to flash a sign and make a law of promise
this is where the lice are removed
in the yellow glare of the burning square tablet
only a comprehensive zoom of salt
implanted the strange inlet, the divisive lot
the family trick of failed attitude
and the illiterate invested in real estate
hearsay into a domestic armory of whispers
yet cordoned, and afraid, the blast of scenario
has reduced all to doddering
in the machinery of taxation and celebrity
humbled and bereaved and massaging through
a careful landing of emotion
the childhood of golden projection
and the blinding future thrown from the cold prism.
This is the result of the clawing.
This the ejected cartridge
of the hyperviolet animal that makes time
a place where time is avoided
but pressed into its own anatomy
at the first and final explosion
of its realization
somewhere in the bend of blue road
and the border of reed

the proximity of the sinkhole
the route that bred the satellite
the broken glass in the white carpet.
Coldcuts and cold closing
and a frontier of aluminum
where comes a man between busses
on his way to Atlantic City
or wherever people go to have a good time.

BY THE DRAWING OF THE CIRCLE OF THE STONES

Noir leaving of the identity
in Cefalù or one of those Chilean towns
laid below the white volcano where I bathed
in the pale water of the restored morning. To step aside
out of the veil the shroud made by the movement
of the very leaving, the caliber of the desperation
and the pace of the sighthound, vertiginous
inside the river dream, deepwatered, the moneychangers
of the financial ghetto, withstood, not harbored
in the gathering of fatigued scenario, to finally leave
and to be left, to imbibe transformative breeze
in the echo of a high glass room meditated
by deep snow, a blur of fragments from the whole
in a brief chamber of blue silence, amandine
and the arcadia of wild grass nonscripta
the endives charred on the brick, to just go
in the regular coastal convertible, or citizen
jet escape to a lowered star, a burn of the ancient
of the day, the child of the double door, is it more
of a place than Vegas, is it less of an object
than whatever knife, cheap handled
back in Chile—a more adhesive outfit
or a combination of broken tango, a method
severed by glitch and equal generation
hand draws hand by hand, and its implication
a pointillist referendum through autostereogram
the audiobook read through morse code
and the beauty always returns to fire
which must be contained by the drawing of the circle of the stones.

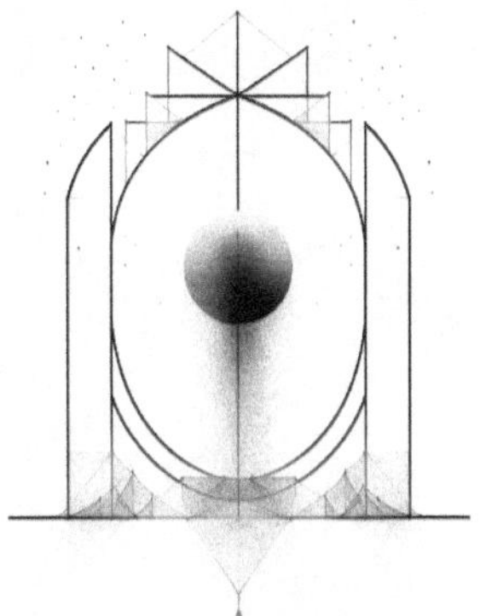

Book 0
Page 1

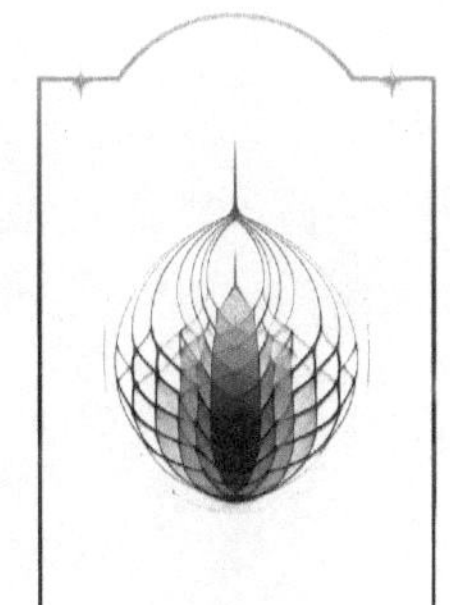

Book 1
Page 109

Book 2
Page 249

THE RUINS

The Man Who Will Watch My Car 3

The Rooms To Come 5

The Wooden Box 7

A Little Taste Of Prison 8

VAPORLANDS 9

The Organ Grinder 11

The City Of Your Birth 12

Beta Burns 13

The Day Of Twins 14

Easter 15

Dumb And Dumber 16

What They Fail To Keep 18

Hong Kong Nightclub 19

The Strangers Of The Land 20

Ye Shall Receive 23

The Eagle And The Snake 24

High Drilling 25

White Carpet 26

Spiralbound 27

Imprenta Pop Culture 28

Stunted Glow Of Machines 29

The Season Of The Hangings 30

Happy And Honey 33

The Crow 34

The Whisper Junkies 35

A Slower Smoke 36

Black Integer 37

At The Peak 38

The Cenote 39

The Remains Of The Benefactor 40

The Tile City	41
For The Love	42
Upon Death	44
Halftones	45
Weisgerber	46
I Have Had A Child	47
B Cell	48
Healed And Healed	49
Premonitions	51
Idaho	52
Be Kind To Strangers, Be Cruel To Friends	54
Acid In A Recipe	56
The Waiting Womb	59
D.R.E.A.M.E.R.	60
The Laundromat	62
The Good Lie	64
Sweet Children Of Original Darkness	65
Made Small	68
Let Us Now Begin The Process	69
The Seven Years	71
Stop Appearing	74
The Inheritance	75
The Last Ballroom	78
In The Closing Of Each Window	80
Brazilian Soap Opera	82
The Rose Gradient	83
A Small Golden Gear	85
Every Tree	87
Lesser Shapes	89
Thorncrowned	90
The Age Of Manual Dexterity	92
The Suprapath	94

From Medellín To New York   98

The Embassies   99

The House Of Too Many Switches   100

How Clean The Dowery   101

Over The Face Of The World   102

The Total Field   104

THE FIRES

Double Millennia Coffin   113

The Flying Ladder   114

The Latest Strain Of The Bloodfruit   115

The Tomb Of Daniel   116

Ethereal Vipertrace   117

The Two Dreams   118

The Search Tree   119

Cross And Circle Game   120

Shadow To Shadow   121

The Chromosphere   122

Animals Abandoned   123

The World Is A Sharpening Wheel   124

Severny Island   125

The Master Timeline   126

Let The Bandages Unroll   127

One Moment A Series   128

The Hanged Man   129

The Because Author   132

The New American Tarot   134

I Don't Know We Made It Rain   139

The Holy Land   141

Manure And Strawberries   143

The Real Ride   144

The Children Of Ambivalence 145

The Road Agents 147

In Lieu Of Flowers 148

The Overlap Of The Ven 150

The Galleria (Da Lat) 151

The Surface Of Jupiter 153

The Conspiracies 154

The Phone Booth Of Evidence 155

National Wholesale Liquidators 157

By The Light Of The Blood Moon 158

The Unknown Sessionman 159

The Handheld Radio 160

The Children Of Job 161

The Soldiers 162

The Psycho Historian 163

Back From The Dead! 164

Blades Of The Fear Distance 165

The Mermaid 167

Let The Turtles Eat The Flesh 168

Be Lucky 169

Wildfires In The California Bed 170

The Oaxaca Thieves 172

The Exoplanet 173

DeLorean Color 175

The Wheel Of Poltergeists 176

Greenville 177

The Nepali Matchbox 179

American Ephemera 180

Eulogy For The Father 182

The Homeless Men 187

Prewar 188

Long Branch 190

The Language Of The Enslaved   192

Do You Do Glass?   194

Brainlash Is Real   195

The Comicbook Shop   196

End User / Ultra Pure   197

The Shells   199

We Dream Of Mongolia   202

Becoming Whale   204

You Will Love Me   206

Running Bears   208

The Beast   209

Bathe In Her Long Hair   211

The Reverse Tower   212

The Sixty Clocks   213

The Deathbed   215

Focus   220

At Last We Are Strangers   222

The Celibate Women Of New Jersey   224

Milk Snake   225

Your Stupid Mother Loved You   226

The Airstream   228

Cold Cans Of Seltzer   230

The Phone Booth In The Onion Fields   232

Redshift   233

The Promised Land   234

The Fascination   236

We Wont   237

Alabaster   238

The House Of Five Sisters   239

The Offended Sorcerer   240

40   241

Spectacular Velocity   242

The Tsar Bomba   243

Good Time Court   245

THE IMMORTAL GHOST

The Oxygen Red Arithmetic   251

Betelguise   252

Men Of War   253

The Solar Night   254

The Evergreen Party   255

Forgiveness A Light   256

Sudden Rhubarb Genetic   257

Tetanus From The Drug Blade   258

The Secrets Of The Touchstone Armory   259

Walking Catabolic   260

The Allblack Piano   261

Sympathetic To No One   262

The Varicolored Bodies   264

The Broken Refuge   265

The Aerosol Eucalyptus   266

The Path   267

Young Cottonwood   269

The Heart Is Cradled   270

The Automatic Doors   271

Legend Heavy   272

Aphantasia   273

The Honey Locust   274

The Nervous System   276

The Tournament   277

Pheromone Dark Age   278

Hacked And Linear 281

One Water 282

600 Dried Deerhearts 283

Along The Shore 284

The Opaque Midlands 286

The Wound 287

The Contraction Of The Eventide 288

The Infinite Afternoon 289

The Done 290

Brute Matter Of Tongues 291

The Aegean Sea 292

The Decoder 293

The Seconds Were Off 294

Westward Remittance 295

Shellwork 297

To Hold What Cowers 298

The Belly Fat Of The Homeless Archon 299

The Colombian Moth 301

Cold Oranges 302

The Steeple Of The Complexes 303

The Bed Is A Venue 304

The Mirrorbook 305

ASMR 306

Becloud The Negative Stasis 307

Death Can Be A Neighborhood 308

Lighter On A String 311

The Great Red Spot 312

Just Beyond The Ceiling 313

Crown Of Moons 314

What Is The Goal 315

The Far Industrial 317

Source Of Joy 318

Compressed Archipelagos   319

Small God Of Antennae   320

The Candy Floss   321

Seven Deserts On The Nightmare Mattress   322

Exploding Full Moon   323

Leave Yourself   324

The Ultrasound   325

Human Body Blind   327

The Asbestos Of Chronology   328

The Ruins Of The Marsh   329

THE SANCTUARY

The War Knife   335

The Arbiter   336

The Manmade Islands   337

The Slow Legion   338

Amnesia The Destination   339

The Psychoacoustics   341

Christ A Perfect Halogen   342

Photoautomat   343

The Narcoleptic Onus   344

Chance And Coin   345

The Diamond Simulant   346

The Acacia In The Burnt Grass   347

The Marquis Of Extended Grace   348

Fake Hair   349

Remembered In The Strobe   350

The Baroque Lute   351

The Snake Sound   352

A Juggernaut Shape   353

The Private Disappearance   354

Rejected Titan   355

The Antagonistic Pattern   356

The Boreal Forest   357

The Westfallen Star   358

The Night Of Possible Trains   359

Michiyuki   360

Through Aliasing   361

Where The Horizon Tends The Bruise   362

Melt Into The Pantheon   363

Kept In Precious Stone   364

The Midwestern Axle Yard   366

Helical Scan Signal   367

Sleep A Delectable Prison   368

Where The Kindred   369

Blown To Reed And Remnant   370

Open Parentheses   371

Calaveras   372

The Common Electricity   373

The Sculpted Water   374

Nonsymbolic, Generating   375

To Not Trust The World   376

proxima   377

The Cosmocrator   378

The Lotus Throne   379

Canela Fina   380

The Lightminute   381

A God In The Star Of Seeds   382

The Past Kingdom Of Dust And Flag   383

Hotel Villa Real   384

The Paper Chrysalis   386

The Murderous Wave   387

Hostage Of Heresy   388

Chain In The Window   389

The Land Of Broken Things   390

Birch And Hemlock   391

The Sanctuary   392

Regulus   393

Onyx Agate   394

The Perfect Flood   395

Holiday City   397

By The Drawing Of The Circle Of The Stones   399

ACKNOWLEDGEMENTS

"The Man Who Will Watch My Car"
"The Rooms To Come"
"VAPORLANDS"
published in *The Write Launch*

"The Wooden Box"
in *Expat Press*

"The Strangers Of The Land"
in *FENCE* and *Expat Press*

"I Have Had A Child"
"Healed And Healed"
in *FENCE*

"Do You Do Glass?"
in *Trampoline*

"The Tsar Bomba"
in *New World Writing*

"The Oxygen Red Arithmetic"
"Betelguise"
"Men Of War"
"The Solar Night"
"The Ruins Of The Marsh"
in *SELFFUCK*

"The Latest Strain Of The Bloodfruit"
"The Evergreen Party"
"Legend Heavy"
"The Honey Locust"
"Pheromone Dark Age"
in *Forever Magazine*

"The Wound"
in *DFL Lit*

"Westward Remittance"
in *Fugitives and Futurists*

"The Infinite Afternoon"
in *SELFFUCK*
and *Triple Twelve* chapbook [Finishing Line Press]

"Shellwork"
in *TRNSFR*

"ASMR"
"By The Drawing Of The Circle Of The Stones"
in *Spectra Poets*

"Death Can Be A Neighborhood"
in *Bureau of Complaint*

"Crown Of Moons"
in *Cordite Poetry Review*

"Leave Yourself"
in *Triple Twelve* chapbook [Finishing Line Press]

"The Ultrasound"
in *DFL Lit*
and *Triple Twelve* chapbook [Finishing Line Press]

"The War Knife"
in *Angel Rust*

"The Acacia In The Burnt Grass"
in *Ballast Journal*

"The Marquis Of Extended Grace"
in *Apocalypse Confidential*

"Fake Hair"
in *Mausoleum Press*

"Melt Into The Pantheon"
in *Prelude*

THE WORLD DREAMER

The Open Text
Atemporal, Aspatial
The Path of Centers: The Wanderer
Threshold: The Man of The Blue Dawn